Little Bead Boxes

Little Bead Boxes

JULIA S. PRETL

12 Miniature Boxes Built with Beads

Creative Publishing
international

Minneapolis, MN

© 2006 Creative Publishing international, Inc.
Text and illustrations © 2006 Julia S. Pretl

Creative Publishing
international

Creative Publishing international, Inc.
400 First Avenue North, Suite 300
Minneapolis, Minnesota 55401
1-800-328-3895
www.creativepub.com

Photographer: Allan Penn
Cover & Book Design: Deborah Fillion
Illustrations: Julia S. Pretl

Library of Congress Cataloging-in-Publication Data
Pretl, Julia S.
    Little bead boxes : 12 miniature boxes built with beads / Julia S. Pretl.
        p. cm.
    ISBN 1-58923-291-7 (pbk.)
    1. Beadwork. 2. Ornamental boxes. 3. Miniature craft. I. Title.
    TT860.P74 2006
    745.58'2—dc22   2006010449
                                                        CIP
ISBN-13: 978-1-58923-291-4 (pbk)
ISBN-10: 1-58923-291-7 (pbk)

Printed in Singapore
10 9 8 7 6

This book is dedicated to the box beaders, who applauded me for the fun parts, yelled at me for the difficult parts, and made many suggestions to help me improve my instructions. I thank you all.

This book is the result of many hours spent designing, redesigning, teaching—and making boxes, boxes, and more boxes. With nearly every box I make, I discover a slightly easier way to accomplish one part or another.

I made my first beaded box in 1992. I had grown tired of making amulet purses, and I was looking for a bigger project.

I remembered one particular amulet bag in which I had decreased the corners so that the bottom was relatively flat—and I decided to expand on this idea. My end product was a triangular purse about 4½" (11.4 cm) high with a lid and a braided strap. I discovered later that I could also make a triangular purse in square stitch and a square purse, too.

Years later, I was asked to teach a class on my beaded purses. Because I felt that it was important to offer several different options to my students, I set out to find a formula for beading five- and six-sided purses.

I experimented by making 2" (5.1 cm) models of each shape, and, as I worked, I found that by increasing the tension of my thread and reducing the size, I had created a wonderful, tiny box! Inspired, I beaded a lid for my little box and then embellished it by adding a handle and feet made from lampworked beads.

Thanks to the encouragement of my friends at home and the incredible beading community that has come together on the Web, I gathered the courage to write this book.

I hope that you enjoy creating these little treasures as much as I do!

Contents

PATTERNS FOR HEXAGON BOXES

PATTERNS FOR PENTAGON BOXES

PATTERNS FOR SQUARE BOXES

Getting Started

My little boxes are self-supporting, peyote-stitched vessels, woven with cylinder beads. I developed this technique by applying to beadwork the same principles that are used to increase in crochet. These boxes may be as small as 1" (2.5 cm) wide—or as large as your patience (and tension) will allow.

The process of making a box has many steps. As you complete each step, write down what you have done in case you need to refer back later in the project.

Before you begin a new step, read through that section carefully. There are several instances in which the instructions differ for different types of boxes. There may also be important or helpful notes to help you work.

Study the diagrams carefully, and make sure that your beadwork structure conforms to the diagram before you proceed to the next row.

There are patterns and instructions for twelve boxes, three of each of the four shapes: triangle, hexagon, pentagon, and square. There are also instructions for two oblong variations. The patterns and instruction sections have been arranged from the easiest box to build (triangle) to the more complex (square), but you may begin with any of the four box shapes. Whichever you choose, you will begin making each box at the center of the base.

Tools and Materials

To make bead boxes, you'll need the following materials and supplies. Each project in the book has its own materials list, which will give you the number and size of the beads for that project. Each box is made with multiple colors (coded in the instructions as color A, B, C, D, and so on). All bead counts are approximate, so it's a good idea to buy extra.

- Size 11 cylinder beads (I use Miyuki Delicas)
- Size 12 or smaller beading needles
- Bead thread (such as Silamide or GSP fishing line)
- Large, decorative beads (for the feet and finials)
- Size 11 round seed beads
- Needle-nose pliers

When I first began teaching, I strongly encouraged my students to work with Silamide, a bonded nylon thread, and I used it for every box I made. Since then I have fallen in love with the new GSP fishing lines, such as Fireline, Powerpro, and Spiderwire. Every class I teach inevitably has at least one diehard Nymo user. I finally stopped arguing and learned that, although Nymo will not allow for the amount of tension I like to have in my own boxes, it will still result in a lovely box.

I sometimes like to double my thread so that if one strand breaks, I can make repairs with the piece still intact. I suggest using a thinner thread if you plan to double it and a thicker thread (or fishing line) if you plan to use a single strand. Begin each box with at least 5' (1.5 m) of thread.

Matte cylinder beads (especially black ones) and metallic cylinder beads are much more fragile than coated (shiny) ones. To avoid breakage, I suggest that you use the more durable, coated beads for your first project.

The Basic Parts of the Box

Before you begin to bead, it helps to have an overview of the basic parts and to visualize the steps involved in building each one.

The Base

The first step is making the base, or bottom. There are four different base shapes: triangular, hexagonal, pentagonal, and square. Generally, the base will be relatively

a. Flat lid fits
inside box

b. Lid fits
over sides

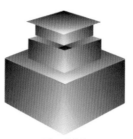

c. Flat lid fits
in recessed top

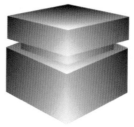

d. Lid fits over
recessed top

e. Small lid over
recessed top

flat, but, depending on the shape you are making and the tension as you work, the base may have a tendency to peak in the center.

The hexagonal base has a pronounced peak. When the base is inverted—so that the peak is inside the box—the six corners of the box base and body are sharp. The hexagonal peaked base also can be used, peak side out, as a domed lid. The bases of pentagonal boxes always lie perfectly flat. The bases of triangle and square boxes can vary.

The Sides

The next step in building a box is making the sides. The sides consist of a single straight tube of beadwork that is built up directly from the base.

As the sides of your box approach the desired height, you have the option of creating two different types of top edges: straight or recessed. A straight top is simply an extension of the sides of the box. A recessed top is a bit more complicated, but the result is especially attractive.

To decide which type of top edge to make, it is important to understand the relationship between the tops of the box sides and the box lid. The two styles of box top—straight or recessed—accommodate different styles of lids.

A straight top is designed to accommodate:

- A flat lid with inner walls that fit inside the box (a)
- A lid with sides that fit over the sides of the box (b)

A recessed top is designed to accommodate:

- A flat lid that is smaller than the base of the box with inner walls that fit inside the inner column (the recessed portion of the sides) (c)
- A lid that is the same width as the box with sides that fit over the inner column (d)
- A lid that is smaller than the box with sides that fit over the inner column (e)

The Hem

To finish both straight and recessed tops, you need to create a hem. The hem is a narrow strip of peyote stitch added just inside the top edge of the box. It will eventually "zip" to the outer layer, creating the appearance of a continuous fabric. The hem is truly the most important aspect of this technique. It defines the corners and helps the box to keep its shape.

The Lid

After the body of the box is complete, you will make the lid. There are two types of lids: flat lids (a, c) and lids with sides (b, d, e).

Lids will vary in size, depending on the size of the box and the style of the lid.

Glossary of Terms

Here is a list of some basic terms you will encounter as you work through the instructions to create your box.

Corner bead: The bead that forms a point in the base or lid, created by making consistent increases at the outer edges of each base or lid segment. For example, a triangle base has three corner beads; a square base has four corner beads.

Down bead: Every bead in the row prior to the working row. Down beads will recede into the edges of the beadwork.

Hem: A second layer of beads built into the top edge of the sides to add stability and shape to the box.

Inner column: A tube of peyote stitch made after decreasing the sides of the box. The inner column is narrower than the box sides and often helps to seat the lid.

Inner walls: An unhemmed tube of beadwork, built from the underside of a flat box lid. The inner walls slide into the sides of the box to keep the lid securely seated on the box.

Stepping up: The process of sewing again into the last bead from the previous row to begin a new row.

Up bead: Every bead in the working row. Up beads will protrude from the edges of the beadwork.

Building a Box

Building the Base

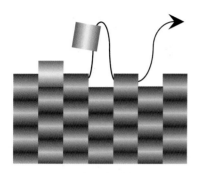

New bead added
between up beads

To build the boxes, you will work with variations on peyote stitch. Peyote stitch is a popular beadwork technique that has several variations. A more descriptive name for the stitch is "one-bead netting," because technically it is a netted stitch with "up" beads—the beads that protrude from the row—and "down" beads—the beads that recede into the row. The working row is always built from the up beads. The netting contains one bead per stitch, so the result is a solid fabric of beads.

To make the boxes, you will work with two basic beadwork variations on peyote stitch: circular peyote stitch and tubular peyote stitch. You don't need to have experience with these beadwork stitches. By following the written instructions and drawings provided, you will be learning these techniques naturally.

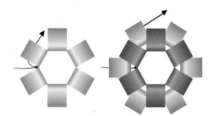

Circular peyote stitch

Circular peyote stitch begins at a center point and increases symmetrically, allowing each row to have a greater number of beads than the row before it, so that the beadwork radiates outward. The planned increases create segments in the beadwork and give each box shape its specific number of sides.

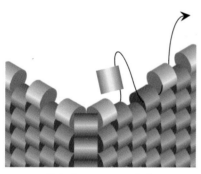

Tubular peyote stitch

Tubular peyote stitch begins at a top or a bottom edge and creates a beaded tube. Box sides are formed with tubular peyote stitch. If you begin tubular peyote with an odd number of beads, the rows of beadwork spiral. If you begin with an even number of beads, the first bead in a row is also the last bead, so you need to "step up"—or sew again into the last bead—to begin the next row.

To make the base, you will work with the variation on circular peyote. To get comfortable with the technique, you'll want to practice first. Here are the instructions for making the base for each of the four box shapes. Choose the shape you'd like to try first as your practice piece, and follow the instructions for that box shape.

Begin with a length of thread approximately 5' (1.5 m) long and about 5 grams of beads in one or more colors that you like. I prefer to double my thread (10' [3 m] long before doubling) so that if one strand breaks, I can make repairs with the piece still intact—but do whatever is comfortable for you. I suggest that you use a thinner thread if you plan to double it and a thicker thread if you plan to use a single strand.

Triangle Box
STARTUP ROWS

Row 1: String 3 beads, and tie in an overhand knot (as if you are beginning to tie a shoestring), leaving an 8" (20.3 cm) tail. Grasp the tail tightly in the hand that is not holding the needle until you have established several rows. Sew through the next bead.

Row 2: String 2 new beads, and proceed through the next bead to form a V. Continue adding 2 beads after each bead in the previous row until you reach the end of the row. You will now have 9 beads. "Step up" to begin the next row. (Note: When you step up, you will sew through only the first of the 2 beads, coming out in the center of the V.)

Row 3: String 2 beads, and sew through the second of the 2 beads from the previous row. You should now have a second V inside the first one. String 1 bead, and sew through the next up bead. Pull firmly so that this bead snaps into place.

Continue this process, sewing 2 beads over each corner bead and then 1 bead between each 2 up beads, until you reach the end of the row. Step up to begin the next row. (Note: When you step up, you will sew through only the first of the 2 beads, coming out in the center of the V.)

Startup rows for triangle base

Row 1

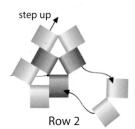

step up

Row 2

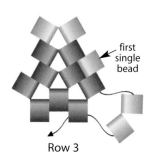

first single bead

Row 3

Making a bead box is a high-tension project. Pull firmly on the thread (not the needle!) after every stitch.

INCREASE CYCLE

By now you have noticed that the base portion of the triangle box is made up of two parts: three corners (where the increases occur) and three straight sides (beaded in typical peyote stitch). After the startup row, each row will increase the triangle by 3 beads (1 bead per side). Continue to add 2 beads to each corner—each V inside the one from the previous row—until your triangle reaches the desired size (about 1" to 1½" [2.5 cm to 3.8 cm] for your practice piece).

Last Row: String 1 bead, and sew through the second of the 2 beads, making sure that it sits snugly inside the V. This bead establishes the corner of the triangle. Sew 1 bead between the up beads until you come out in the center of the next V. Add a bead for the second corner. Continue until you reach the end of the row.

When you have finished the increase cycles, begin making the sides (page 24).

Last Row

Startup rows for hexagon base

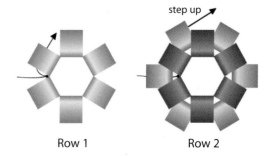

step up

Row 1   Row 2

Hexagon Box

STARTUP ROWS

Row 1: String 6 beads, and tie in an overhand knot (as if you are beginning to tie a shoestring), leaving an 8" (20.3 cm) tail. Grasp the tail tightly in the hand not holding the needle until you have established several rows. Sew through the next bead.

Row 2: String 1 new bead, and proceed through the next bead. You may need to pull the thread firmly to get the new bead to snap between the 2 beads in the previous row.

Continue adding a bead after each bead in the previous row until you reach the end of the row. You will now have 12 beads. Step up to begin the next row.

Row 3: Repeat row 2. You will now have 18 beads. Step up to begin the next row.

Row 4: String 2 beads, and sew through the next bead. This should form a V. String 2 more beads, and sew through the next bead. Continue adding 2 beads after each bead in the previous row until you reach the end of the row. Step up to begin the next row. (Note: When you step up, you will sew through only the first of the 2 beads, coming out in the center of the V.)

Row 5: String 1 bead, and sew through the second of the 2 beads, making sure that it sits snugly inside the V. This bead establishes the corner of the hexagon. String 1 bead, and then sew through the next up bead. Pull firmly so that this bead snaps into place. Add a bead for the second corner. Continue until you reach the end of the row. Step up to begin the next row. (Note: The last bead of the row will be the first leg of the first V, and you will step up to the adjacent corner bead.)

E̲ach time you begin or end a thread, weave the tail into the beadwork by stitching diagonally through adjacent beads. When weaving in the tail, avoid sewing through the corner beads and the beads adjacent to the corner beads. They are the most difficult to repair when broken. You'll find tips for replacing broken beads on page 32.

INCREASE CYCLE

The base portion of the hexagon box is made up of two parts: six corners (where the increases occur) and six straight sides (beaded in flat peyote stitch). As you proceed, the corners increase in cycles. The hexagon box has an increase cycle of three rows, as follows:

Row 1: Bead around the hexagon as usual with 1 bead between every 2 up beads (including the corner bead).

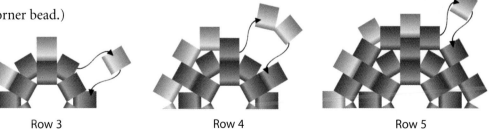

| Row 3 | Row 4 | Row 5 |

Row 2: Add 2 beads to each corner to form a V.

Row 3: Add 1 bead to each corner, inside the V.

After the startup rows, each cycle will increase the hexagon by 6 beads (1 bead per side). Continue this cycle until your hexagon reaches the desired size (about 2" [5.1 cm] for your practice piece).

When you have finished the increase cycles, begin making the sides (page 26).

Startup rows for pentagon base

Row 1

Row 2

Row 3

Row 4

Pentagon Box
STARTUP ROWS

Row 1: String 5 beads and tie in an overhand knot (as if you are beginning to tie a shoestring), leaving an 8" (20.3 cm) tail. Grasp the tail tightly in the hand that is not holding the needle until you have established several rows. Sew through the next bead.

Row 2: String 1 new bead, and proceed through the next bead. You may need to pull the thread firmly to get the new bead to snap between the 2 beads in the previous row. Continue adding a bead after each bead in the previous row until you reach the end of the row. You will now have 10 beads. Step up to begin the next row.

Row 3: String 2 beads, and sew through the next bead. This should form a V. String 2 more beads, and sew through the next bead. Continue adding 2 beads after each bead in the previous row until you reach the end of the row. Step up to begin the next row. (Note: When you step up, you will sew through only the first of the 2 beads, coming out in the center of the V.)

Row 4: String 1 bead, and sew through the second of the 2 beads, making sure that it sits snugly inside the V. This bead establishes the corner of the pentagon. String 1 bead, and then sew through the next up bead. Pull firmly so that this bead snaps into place. Add a bead for the second corner. Continue until you reach the end of the row. Step up to begin the next row. (Note: The last bead of the row will be the first leg of the first V, and you will step up to the adjacent corner bead.)

INCREASE CYCLE

The base portion of the pentagon box is made up of two parts: five corners (where the increases occur) and five straight sides (beaded in flat peyote stitch). As you proceed, the corners increase in cycles. The pentagon box has an increase cycle of four rows, as follows:

Row 1: Bead around the pentagon as usual with 1 bead between every 2 up beads (including the corner bead).

Row 2: This row is new; it is not included in the startup rows. String 3 beads, and proceed through the next bead. The middle bead of these 3 beads should lie directly on top of the

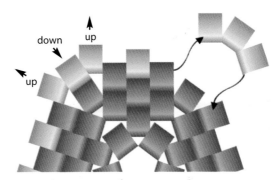

Increase row for pentagon base

one below it. Pull up the side beads, with your fingernails if necessary, to seat the middle one. Continue adding 3 beads to each corner. Step up to begin the next row. (Note: When you step up, you will sew through only the first of the 3 beads.)

Row 3: Add 2 beads to each corner, skipping the middle bead, to form a V.

Row 4: Add 1 bead to each corner, inside the V.

After the startup rows, each cycle will increase the pentagon by 10 beads (2 beads per side). Continue this cycle until your pentagon reaches the desired size (about 2" [5.1 cm] for your practice piece).

When you have finished the increase cycles, begin making the sides (page 26).

Square Box

STARTUP ROWS

Row 1: String 4 beads, and tie in an overhand knot (as if you are beginning to tie a shoestring), leaving an 8" (20.3 cm) tail. Grasp the tail tightly in the hand that is not holding the needle until you have established several rows. Sew through the next bead.

Row 2: String 1 new bead, and proceed through the next bead. Continue adding a bead after each bead in the previous row until you reach the end of the row. You will now have 8 beads. Step up to begin the next row.

Row 3: String 3 beads, and proceed through the next bead. The middle bead of these 3 should lie directly on top of the one below it. Pull up the side beads, with your fingernails if necessary, to seat the middle one. Continue adding 3 beads after each bead in the previous row until you reach the end of the row. Step up to begin the next row. (Note: When you step up, you will sew through only the first of the 3 beads.)

Row 4: String 2 beads, and sew through the third bead of the three-bead set from the previous row, skipping the middle bead to form a V. String 1 bead, and sew through the next up bead. Pull firmly so that this bead snaps into place. Continue this process—sewing 2 beads over each corner bead and then 1 bead between every two up beads—until you reach the end of the row. Step up to begin the next row. (Note: When you step up, you will sew through only the first of the 2 beads, coming out in the center of the V.)

Row 5: String 2 beads, and sew through the second of the two beads from the previous row. You should now have a second V sitting inside the first one. Sew 1 bead between the up beads until you come out in the center of the next V. Add 2 beads for the second corner. Continue until you reach the end of the row. Step up to begin the next row.

Startup rows for
square base

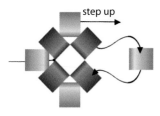

Row 1

Row 2

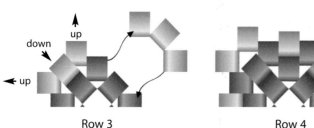

Row 3

Row 4

(Note: When you step up, you will sew through only the first of the two beads, coming out in the center of the V.)

Row 6: String 1 bead, and sew through the second of the two beads, making sure that it sits snugly inside the V. This bead establishes the corner of the square. Sew 1 bead between the up beads until you come out in the center of the next V. Add a bead for the second corner. Continue until you reach the end of the row. Step up to begin the next row. (Note: The last bead of the row will be the first leg of the first V, and you will step up to the adjacent corner bead.)

INCREASE CYCLE

By now you have noticed that the base portion of the square box is made up of two parts: four corners (where the increases occur) and four straight sides (which have no increases). As you proceed, the corners increase in cycles. The square box has an increase cycle of five rows, as follows:

Row 1: Bead around the square as usual, with 1 bead between every 2 up beads (including the corner bead).

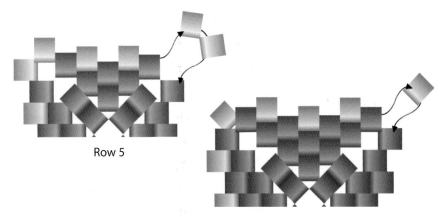

Row 5

Row 6

Row 2: Add 3 beads to each corner, making sure that the middle bead touches the bead below it.

Row 3: Add 2 beads to each corner, skipping the middle bead, to form a V.

Row 4: Add 2 beads to each corner, forming a second V inside the first one.

Row 5: Add 1 bead to each corner, inside the second V.

After the startup rows, each cycle will increase the square by 12 beads (3 beads per side). Continue this cycle until your square reaches the desired size (about 2" [5.1 cm] for your practice piece).

When you have finished the increase cycles, begin making the sides (page 28).

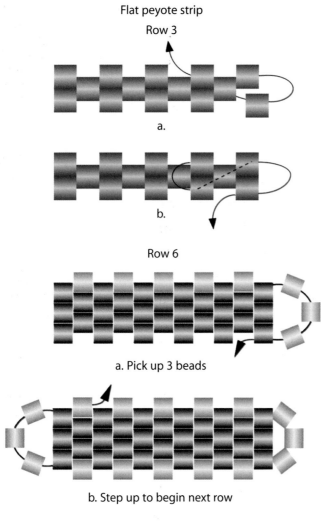

Flat peyote strip

Row 3

a.

b.

Row 6

a. Pick up 3 beads

b. Step up to begin next row

Row 7

Oblong Variations

You can also build an oblong box, working with the square or hexagon base and creating two elongated sides. The sides can be as long as you want.

When making the base for an oblong box, you will work in a variation on peyote stitch called flat peyote stitch. Flat peyote stitch may be even count, which means you begin with an even number of beads, or it may be odd count, which means you begin with an odd number of beads. Even-count peyote is naturally asymmetrical, and odd-count peyote is symmetrical from side to side. To make an oblong box, you will work a strip of flat, odd-count peyote stitch.

ROWS 1 AND 2: String an odd number of beads, as determined by your desired box length. This string of beads will make up the first two rows of the flat peyote strip.

ROW 3: Pick up 1 more bead. Skip the last bead, and sew into the next-to-the-last bead. Skip the next bead in the string, and sew the one that comes after it. Continue this way until you reach the end of the string. This process is identical to tubular peyote stitch. Notice that there is 1 bead remaining. To complete the row, pick up 1 bead, and sew into what is now the last bead in the second row and the next-to-last bead in the first row (a).

Turn the needle 180 degrees to sew into the next-to-last bead of the third row. Then sew through rows 2 and 1 so that the needle exits the last bead of the first row.

Turn the needle again and sew into the last bead of row 3 (b). You are now ready to bead row 4.

ROWS 4 AND 5: Bead by adding 1 bead to each space. Pick up a bead, and sew into the last up bead to begin row 5. Add 1 bead to each space, and finish the row as you did for row 3 (a, b).

ROW 6: Make a sixth row that completely encircles the strip. (Do not turn to begin a seventh row.)

Pick up 3 beads, and sew into the corner bead on the opposite side of the flat edge (a).

Bead a row along the working side of the strip, and add 3 more beads to the remaining flat end. Step up to begin row 7 (b).

Row 7: Bead around the entire edge, this time adding 1 bead between each of the 3 end beads. (You will add a total of 2 beads to each end of the strip.) Step up and follow the instruction for either the hexagon or square variation.

Oblong Hexagon Variation

To make corners on each end for a hexagon box, add 2 beads to each of the three end spaces to establish the increase corners. Bead along the second long side, and repeat this process on the far end. Step up to begin the next row, following the increase cycles for the hexagon box (page 17).

Oblong Square Variation

To make two corners on each end for a square box, add 3 beads to the first end space to establish an increase corner. Add 1 bead to the second end space to establish the short side of the rectangle, and then add 3 more beads to the third end space for the second increase corner. Bead along the second long side; repeat this process for the far end. Step up to begin the next row, following the increase cycles for the square box (page 21).

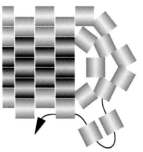

Oblong hexagon variation

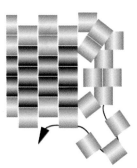

Oblong square variation

Building the Sides

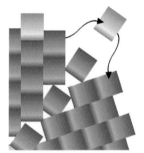

Tubular peyote stitch

When you are satisfied with the size of the base of your box, continue to bead around the edges without increasing (every space gets only one bead). Remember to step up as you complete each row—you are now working with tubular peyote stitch.

After a few rows, you will find that the edges are beginning to curl upward. Keep your tension firm and, as you round the corners, carefully pinch the corner into shape. This is especially important when making a triangle box because the fewer the number of sides, the sharper the corner angle will be.

Straight and Recessed Tops

Depending on the style of the box lid you choose, the sides of your box will be either straight or recessed at the top.

To bead a box that has straight sides from bottom to top, continue until your box is two rows short of the desired height. The last row should have an up bead at the corners. Now you can simply begin to make the hem (page 30).

To bead a box with sides that are recessed at the top, continue until your box is the desired height (about 2" [5.1 cm] for your practice piece). Make one or more decrease cycles, depending on the shape of the box (see sidebar on facing page). A decrease cycle is the opposite of an increase cycle but is identical in appearance.

Decreasing for a Triangle Box

The decrease cycle for a triangle box is simple. After you have completed the first row, every subsequent row is the same.

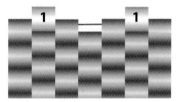

Row 1

Row 2

A complete triangle box decrease cycle is:

Row 1:
Skip the corner bead.

Row 1: Make sure you have finished the sides of your box with an up bead on either side of the corner bead. For the next row, bead the sides as usual. When you come to a corner, omit the corner bead, and sew directly from the first up bead into the next.

Pull firmly on the thread as you sew the first few beads following the skipped bead so that as little thread as possible shows. When you complete this row, the corners of the box will be more defined, and the sides will begin to curl inward. Step up to begin the next row.

Row 2: Bead the next row as you did the first. When you come to a corner, you will notice that the 2 corner beads from the previous row are practically touching. Sew through the first bead and then the next without adding a bead in between. Bead the remaining sides in the same way, skipping a bead as you round each corner. Step up to begin the next row.

When you have finished the required number of decrease cycles for your style of lid, begin making the inner column (page 29).

Decrease Cycles for Sides

Here's an overview of the guidelines to follow when finishing the sides of the box. Each box style will have a different decrease cycle, depending on the style of the lid.

- **For a flat lid that is smaller than the base of the box:**

  All box shapes: Subtract the number of lid increase cycles from the number of base increase cycles. This is the number of decrease cycles you will make.

- **For a lid with sides that are flush with the sides of the box:**

  Triangle box: Complete four decrease cycles.

  Hexagon box: Complete two decrease cycles.

  Pentagon box: Complete one decrease cycle.

  Square box: Complete one decrease cycle.

- **For a lid with sides that are smaller than the base of the box:**

  All box shapes: Subtract the number of lid increase cycles from the number of base increase cycles. This is the number of decrease cycles you will make. Next, follow the directions above for a lid with sides that are flush with the sides of the box.

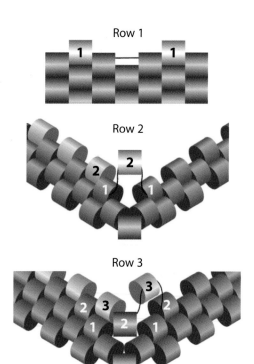

Row 2

Row 3

A complete hexagon box decrease cycle is:

Row 1: Skip the corner bead.

Row 2: Bead as usual (add the corner bead).

Row 3: Bead as usual.

Decreasing for a Hexagon Box

The decrease cycle for a hexagon box includes three rows.

Row 1: Make sure you have finished the sides of your box with an up bead on either side of the corner bead. For the next row, bead the sides as usual. When you come to a corner, omit the corner bead, and sew directly from the first up bead into the next.

Pull firmly on the thread as you sew the first few beads after the skipped bead so

that as little thread as possible shows. When you complete this row, the corners of the box will be more defined, and the sides will begin to curl inward. Step up to begin the next row.

Row 2: Bead this row as usual, with a bead between every pair of up beads.

Row 3: Bead as usual with a bead between every pair of up beads (including those on either side of the corner bead). You have now completed the decrease cycle for the hexagon box.

When you have finished the required number of decrease cycles for your style of lid, begin making the inner column (page 29).

Decreasing for a Pentagon Box

The decrease cycle for a pentagon box includes four rows.

Row 1: Make sure you have finished the sides of your box with an up bead on either side of the corner bead. For the next row, bead the sides as usual. When you come to a corner, omit the corner bead, and sew directly from the first up bead into the next.

Pull firmly on the thread as you sew the first few beads following the skipped bead so that as little thread as possible shows. When you complete this row, the corners of the box will be more defined, and the sides will begin to curl inward. Step up to begin the next row.

Row 2: Bead this row as usual, with a bead between every pair of up beads.

Row 3: Bead the sides of this row as usual, with a bead between every pair of up beads. When you reach a corner, do not sew into the new corner bead from the previous row.

Row 4: Bead as usual with a bead between every pair of up beads (including those on either side of the corner bead). You have now completed the decrease cycle for the pentagon box.

When you have finished the required number of decrease cycles for your style of lid, begin making the inner column (page 29).

Row 1

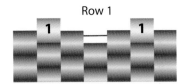

Row 2

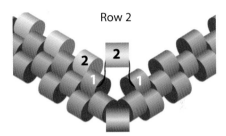

Row 3

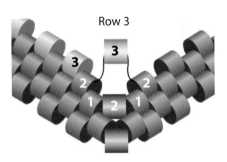

Row 4

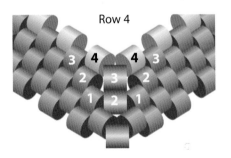

A complete pentagon box decrease cycle is:

Row 1:
Skip the corner bead.

Row 2:
Bead as usual (add the corner bead).

Row 3:
Bead as usual (add the corner bead; do not sew into the corner bead from the previous row).

Row 4:
Bead as usual.

Row 1

1   1

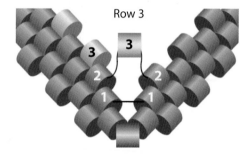

Row 2

2

1   1

Decreasing for a Square Box

The decrease cycle for a square box includes five rows.

Row 1: Make sure you have finished the sides of your box with an up bead on either side of the corner bead. For the next row, bead the sides as usual. When you come to a corner, omit the corner bead, and sew directly from the first up bead into the next.

Pull firmly on the thread as you sew the first few beads following the skipped bead so that as little thread as possible shows. When you complete this row, the corners of the box will be more defined, and the sides will begin to curl inward. Step up to begin the next row.

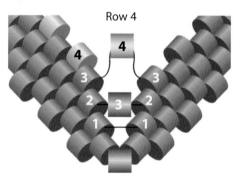

Row 3

3   3
2   2
1   1

> A complete square box decrease cycle is:
>
> Row 1:
> Skip the corner bead.
>
> Row 2:
> Skip the corner bead.
>
> Row 3:
> Bead as usual (add the corner bead).
>
> Row 4:
> Bead as usual (add the corner bead; do not sew into the corner bead from the previous row).
>
> Row 5:
> Bead as usual.

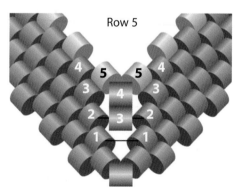

Row 4

4   4
3   3
2   3   2
1   1

Row 5

4   5   5   4
3   4   3
2   3   2
1   1

Row 2: Bead the next row as you did the first. When you come to a corner, sew through the first bead and then the next without adding a bead in between. There will probably be some thread visible between the two beads—that's okay. Bead the remaining sides in the same way, skipping a bead as you round each corner. Step up to begin the next row.

Row 3: Bead this row as usual, with a bead between every pair of up beads, including the corner beads.

Row 4: Bead the sides of this row as usual, with a bead between every pair of up beads. When you reach a corner, do not sew into the new corner bead from the previous row.

Row 5: Bead as usual with a bead between every pair of up beads (including those on either side of the corner bead). You have now completed the decrease cycle for the square box.

When you have finished the required number of decrease cycles for your style of lid, begin making the inner column.

The Inner Column

After you have made the appropriate number of decreases, you will begin the inner column. Bead the next row with tubular peyote stitch, with a bead between every pair of up beads, including the corner beads (a).

(The drawing below shows a recessed top for a hexagon lid, but the inner columns for all the box shapes work the same way.)

The bead rows will begin to curl upward. Continue until the column is two rows short of the desired height. The last row should end with an up bead at each corner (b).

Now you are ready to make the hem.

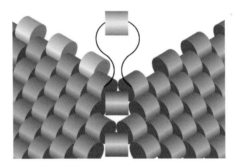

a.

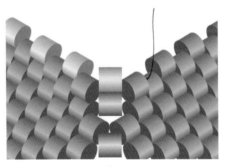

b.

The Hem

Before completing the last two rows of the box, you need to complete four hem rows. To build the first hem row, step back down through the adjacent bead of the previous row so that the needle exits inside the box. Pick up a bead. Sew into the next bead of the same row (a). (This will be much easier to do if you sew diagonally so that the needle exits the outside of the box.)

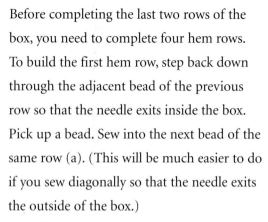

a.

d.

Pull the thread tightly so that the bead sits inside the box and adjacent to the corresponding bead of the last row. Pull the thread so that it slides between the beads and is once again positioned inside the box (b).

Continue to bead around the inside of the box. When you reach the corner, sew into the corner bead of the box and then back down into the adjacent bead without adding a hem bead (c). Repeat this process for each side/corner until you reach the first hem

b.

e.

bead. Sew into this bead to step up for the next hem row.

Add a second row to the hem, filling in each corner space with a single bead (d). Pull the thread tightly as you round each corner to decrease the amount of visible thread—this will sharply define the corner of the box.

Step up and bead a third hem row (e). Step up to bead the last hem row. Add 2 beads to each corner space. When this row is complete, weave through the hem beads until you are able to sew back into the last row of the body to the outside of the box. Complete the body by beading the last two rows (f).

c.

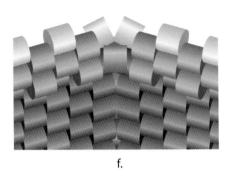

f.

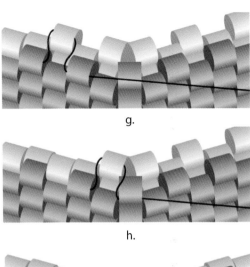

g.

h.

i. The completed hem

You will now "zip"—or interlock—the last row of the body and the last row of the hem. Look at the space where the thread has exited. Behind this space, there will be an up hem bead. Sew into this bead and then into the next up bead of the body of the box (g). Pull the thread tightly so that the hem bead fills the space.

When you reach the corner of the box, sew into only the first of the doubled hem beads and then into the corner bead of the body of the box (h). Pull tight so that the hem bead fills the space beside the corner bead. Sew into the second doubled hem bead, and proceed as usual.

When the hem and the body of the box are completely zipped (i), finish by weaving the thread into the box.

Replacing Broken Beads

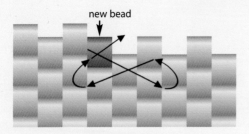

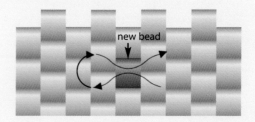

Because making a beaded box is a high-tension project, inevitably you will encounter the problem of broken beads. Although broken beads are frustrating, you can replace them.

As you are beading, if you break a bead in the previous row, string a new bead (preferably one slightly smaller than the space), and sew diagonally through the two adjacent beads in the previous two rows. Exit inside the box to hide the thread.

Next, sew into the bead directly above the bead that you exited and then diagonally through the two adjacent beads in the two previous rows, again exiting inside the box. Sew back into the new bead, and continue beading the row you are working.

If you break a bead when weaving into the beadwork to begin or end a thread, string a new bead (preferably one slightly smaller than the space occupied by the broken bead). Then sew through the bead in the row adjacent to the broken bead. Exit inside the box to hide the thread. Next, sew through the bead directly above the one that you just exited, and then sew back into the new bead. Continue weaving the thread into the beadwork.

When beading a box base or lid, a broken corner bead or a bead beside a corner is nearly impossible to replace. As you are beading a new row, if you break a corner bead in the previous row, take out all the beads until you reach the broken bead. Replace the bead, and bead the row again. (To be on the safe side, do not weave thread ends through the corners of the beadwork when you are beginning or ending a thread.)

Lids, Finials, and Feet

The final step in making a box is to top it with a lid. There are two lid variations: a flat lid and a lid with sides. A flat lid may be the same width as the top of the box or it can extend beyond the edges. A lid with sides may overlap the sides of the box or sit on top.

Flat Lid

A flat lid has an inner wall that fits inside the hem of the box. Bead the top of the lid in the same way as you beaded the base of the box. For a box with a straight top, use the exact same number of increase cycles. For a box with a recessed top, subtract the number of decrease cycles at the top from the number of increase cycles that you made for the base (see sidebar, page 25).

Inner Wall

As you work, check the size of the lid. When the lid no longer clears the edges of the box hem—but before it reaches its full size—you will not step up to begin the next row. Instead, pick up a bead, and sew into the next bead of this same row (just as you did when you added the hem to the body of the box), as shown in the drawing. Again, this is easiest to do if you sew diagonally through each bead so that you exit on the "wrong" side, or underside, of the lid and then bring the thread back to the right side (top side) again.

Continue to add beads in this way until you reach a corner.

There are two types of corners that you will encounter: a corner with a corner bead and a corner without a corner bead, depending on the arrangement of beads in the last row of your increase cycle.

Beading the inner wall

Corner with a Bead

When your needle exits the last bead of the side of the lid, you may find that this row has a bead in the corner. Pick up a bead, sew into the first bead of the next segment of the lid and continue as before (a). When the row is complete, step up to the first inner-wall bead to begin a second row. Bead the second row as usual (b).

Corner without a Bead

When your needle exits the last bead of the side of the lid, you may find that this row has no bead in the corner. Sew into the first bead of the next segment, and continue as before (a). When the row is complete, step up to the first inner wall bead to begin a second row.

Bead the second row as usual. When you exit the last bead of a segment, pick up

Corner with a bead

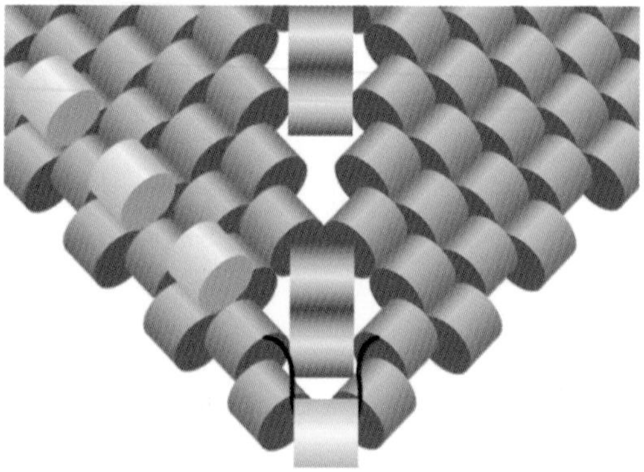

a.

Corner without a bead

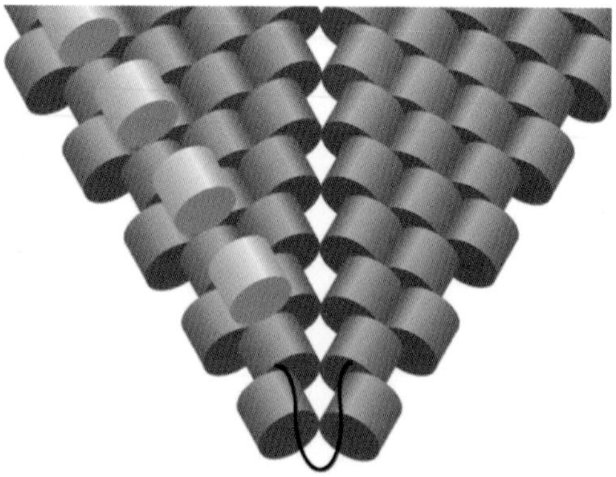

a.

b.

b.

1 bead, and sew into the first bead of the next segment. Bead the rest of the row, adding a bead to each corner (b).

Finishing the Lid

Continue to bead in tubular peyote stitch until the inner wall is approximately $\frac{1}{4}$" (6 mm) deep—it should seat securely in the box top. If you find that the inner wall is catching the side of your box, taper it slightly by skipping each corner space when you bead the last row or by completing the final row with size 15 seed beads. Weave your thread back down to the last lid row. Complete the last two rows.

Lid with Sides

A lid with sides is designed to fit over the opening of a straight top or over the inner column of a box with a recessed top. A lid with sides is beaded in exactly the same way as the body of a box that has a straight top, although the lid usually has shorter sides.

If the lid is to fit over a box with a straight top, make the top of the lid the same size as the base of the box, and then bead:

- Four additional increase cycles for a triangle box

Lid with sides that fit over straight top of pentagon box

- Two additional increase cycles for a hexagon box
- One additional increase cycle for a pentagon box
- One additional increase cycle for a square box

If the sides of the lid are to be flush with the sides of the body of your box, make the same number of increases in the top of the lid as you did in the base of the box (pages 14–21).

Lid with sides smaller than body of square box with recessed top

Finial

a.

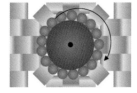

b.

If the lid is to be smaller than the body of your box, subtract one or more full increase cycles for the lid from the number of increase cycles used for the base of the box. This number should correspond to the number of decrease cycles used when making a recessed top (page 25).

Finials

To finish the lid of your box, you may want to add a large, decorative bead to make a knob, or finial. Begin a new thread so that it exits a bead in the center of the top of the lid. String the large bead, and then string a smaller bead. Sew back into the large bead, and exit through the center of the underside of the lid. Sew through another center bead, up through the large bead, and through the center bead again (a).

Repeat this process until you have sewn through each center bead at least once or until the finial is securely attached to the lid. Push the needle back through to the top of the lid, but do not sew through the large bead.

Wind the thread around the base of the large bead several times. The thread should be sandwiched between the large bead and the top of the lid. String enough beads to encircle the base of the large bead, and wrap the thread around it. (I find that round seed beads are much more attractive than cylinder beads here.) Wind the thread around the large bead several more times so that it vanishes between the circle of beads and the top of the lid (b). Weave the thread into the lid to finish.

Feet

To make decorative feet for your box, select 3 or 4 larger beads, depending on the shape of your box. Begin a new thread so that it exits about $\frac{1}{4}$" (6 mm) from one corner of the underside of the box, through a space

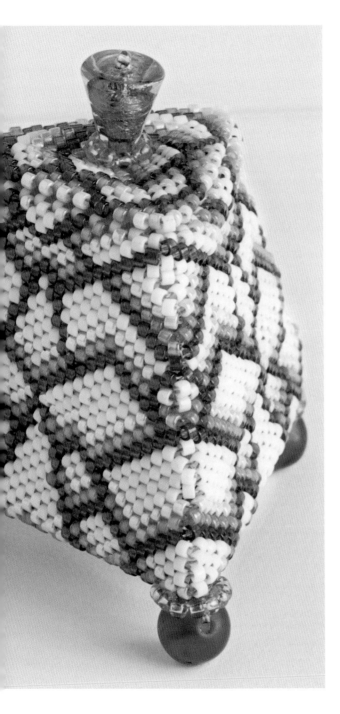

You may find it easier to attach the feet to the base of the box before you begin to construct the sides.

created when you made your increases. String one of the large beads, and then insert the needle through an increase space that is closer to the corner of the box (a). Working from inside the box, push the needle back through the increase space that you originally exited. Repeat this process several times.

As you did with the finial, wind the thread around the base of the large bead several times. The thread should be sandwiched between the large bead and the base of the box. String enough beads to encircle the base of the large bead, and wrap the string around it. (Again, I prefer round seed beads here.) Wind the thread several more times so that it vanishes between the circle of beads and the base of the box (b). Weave the thread into the lid to finish. Add the rest of the feet to the box in the same way.

Foot

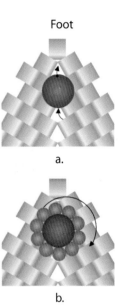

a.

b.

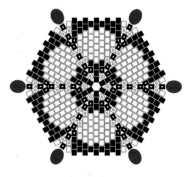

Patterns and Word Maps

In the pattern instructions on pages 43–104, you will find all the information you'll need to make twelve miniature bead boxes—three in each shape: three-sided, four-sided, five-sided, and six-sided. The boxes are arranged by level of complexity—from easiest (triangle box) to most challenging (square box).

The photographs, colored patterns, and coded word maps provide all the information you need to build each box. There's also a list of the materials you'll need and a key so you can easily find the page numbers for the techniques you'll need to refer to as you work.

Pages 105–111 contain blank graph worksheets for each box shape, which you can copy and color to design your own box patterns. You can also download copies of all of the blank graph worksheets from my website, www.darkharebeadwork.com.

Reading Patterns

At first sight, a box pattern can be a bit daunting, but it is not as difficult as it seems. Here are several tips to help you as you read a box pattern.

Box Sides and Lid Sides

Each side of the box is identical, so only one side is shown. Repeat the pattern for each side of the box. Any deviations from this rule are included within the specific pattern.

Side patterns are read from left to right.

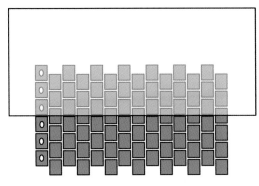

Locating the working row

Choose a side pattern and align the edge of a piece of paper with the top line of one row of beads within the pattern. Notice that the "beads" are staggered. In other words, every other whole bead sits below the edge of the paper. These whole beads constitute the working row. The alternating beads that are cut off at the halfway point belong to the subsequent row.

In the left-hand column of each row of the side pattern is a dotted bead. The dotted bead indicates the corner of the box. (Remember that because peyote stitch is staggered, only every other row has a corner bead.)

Each box-side pattern is read from the bottom row of the graph. You actually begin beading at the bottom row of the box side and will also view your beadwork this way.

Recessed Top

The bottom six rows of the graph at right are tubular peyote, so the corner of every other row receives a bead. The top eight rows, which form the recessed top, contain two decrease cycles. The dotted corner beads represent the new corners created by the decreases. This sample graph is for the side of a pentagon box with a recessed top.

Row 1: Skip the corner bead.

Row 2: Bead as usual (add the corner bead).

Row 3: Bead as usual (add the corner bead; do not sew into the corner bead from the previous row).

Row 4: Bead as usual (no corner bead).

Repeat rows 1 through 4.

Pentagon box side
with recessed top

Bases and Lids

The graphed pattern for the base and the lid of the box begins at the center of the shape. As you increase the number of beads in each segment increases, you read the beads from left to right. As you move to each new

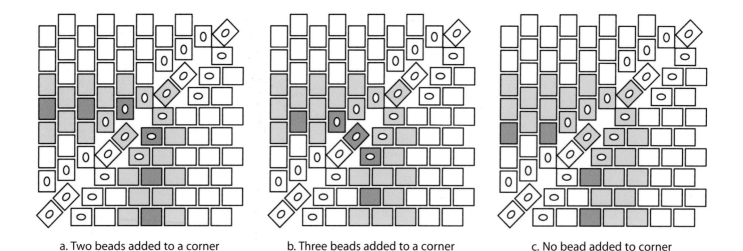

a. Two beads added to a corner

b. Three beads added to a corner

c. No bead added to corner

segment, read around the pattern in a clockwise direction.

In most of the box patterns presented in this book, each segment is identical. In these cases, you do not have to turn the pattern as you work. Simply repeat each graphed segment as many times as the box design requires.

The dotted beads refer to the corner increases. With the exception of the increases, each segment of a base or lid pattern is read in the same way as a box-side pattern.

When you add 2 beads to a corner, the first bead becomes the *last* bead of the segment that you just beaded, and the second bead becomes the *first* bead of the segment that you will bead next (a).

Similarly, when you add 3 beads to a corner, the first bead becomes the *last* bead of the segment that you just beaded, the second bead becomes a *corner* bead, and the third bead becomes the *first* bead of the segment that you will bead next (b).

Finally, notice that for the first row of every increase cycle (except for the triangle box) you will sew through the corner bead in the center of the V from the previous row. No beads are added to the corner (c).

All Patterns

Although every row of the pattern begins at a corner, every row of your beadwork does not. Every time you step up to begin a new row, you are actually sewing through the first bead of the previous row for a second time. For this reason, not only will you move up one pattern row, but also you will move one row to the right. It may be helpful to draw a line that begins with your first bead and moves diagonally up the pattern, as shown in the drawing at right, to keep track of your starting bead on each row.

Reading Word Maps

As a visual person, I have always shunned the idea of word maps. Out of curiosity, I decided to put one of my more complex patterns into text form before I beaded it. I quickly learned how much easier it is to work when you have a pattern in both graphic and written form.

With practice, reading a box pattern will become second nature. Until then, working with both the pattern and the word map together is extremely helpful.

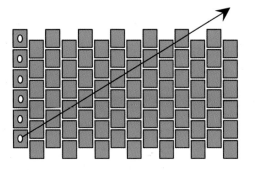

Word maps contain the row number, the bead color (coded as A, B, C, and so on), and the number of beads in that color in the row. Repeats of color combinations are indicated with an **x** and the number of repeats. For example: 1. **C(1)** ... x3 means you will bead one bead of color C three times in row 1.

Here are several tips to help you as you read a word map. Spend some time reading through this section, while referring to your box pattern, before actually beginning to bead.

1. All word maps are read from left to right and top to bottom.
2. The first line of the word map for a box side corresponds to the bottom row of the pattern.
3. The first line of the word map for a base/lid corresponds to the center of the pattern.

When you are building a box, the most important thing to remember is the sequence of the increase cycle for the box that you are beading. This way, you will always know how many beads to add (if any) to each corner.

1. **C(1)** ... x3
2. **C(2)** ... x3
3. **C(2)**; C(1) ... x3
4. **C(2)**; A(1); B(1) ... x3
5. **C(2)**; A(1); C(1); B(1) ... x3
6. **C(2)**; A(2); B(2) ... x3
7. **C(2)**; A(2); C(1); B(2) ... x3
8. **C(2)**; A(3); B(3) ... x3
9. **C(2)**; A(3); C(1); B(3) ... x3
10. **C(2)**; A(4); B(4) ... x3

4. For most box patterns, the sides are identical, so you may start at any corner. (For patterns in which one or more sides are different, such as the New School box on page 66, the specific instructions for the sides are included.)

5. Each row of a base/lid word map begins at the corner of the box—but, because the actual beadwork progresses by one bead per row, you will not always begin a row at the corner. Use the corners as reference points to complete the first partial side of your box. Then continue reading the word map from the corner to the end of the row.

6. Letters describing corner beads are in boldface type and are found at the beginning of the row.

7. When there is more than one corner bead, an increase row is indicated, and all beads listed are to be picked up at the same time. For example, a square base row that begins with *C(3)* is always an increase row. To bead the corner space, you would pick up 3 beads instead of 1, just as you did when increasing for the corner of your practice square (page 20–21).

8. The abbreviation "nc" means "no corner." For rows beginning with "nc," you are sewing into the previous row, which contains a corner bead, so the row on which you are working will have no corner bead.

9. The abbreviation "sc" means "skip corner." This notation indicates a decrease row—so you will sew from the last bead of one side into the first bead of the next without adding a corner bead.

Patterns for
Triangle
Boxes

▲ Kaleidoscope

Finished Size: 2" wide
x 1" tall (5.1 x 2.5 cm)
without finial or feet

A = Light Blue; Delica #747;
584 beads (3 grams)

B = Royal Blue; Delica #726;
480 beads (3 grams)

C = Black; Delica #10;
1,140 beads (6 grams)

Hem/Inner Wall = Any color;
582 beads (3 grams)

A   **B**   **C**

Construction Techniques

For the Base: pages 15–16

For the Sides: pages 24–25

For the Flat Lid: pages 33–35

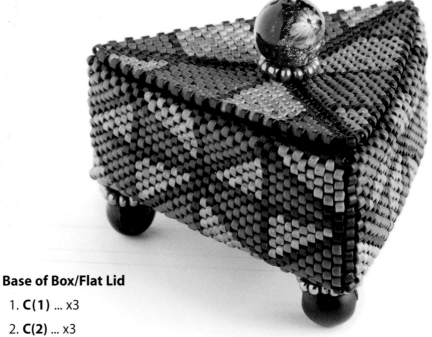

Base of Box/Flat Lid

1. **C(1)** ... x3
2. **C(2)** ... x3
3. **C(2)**; C(1) ... x3
4. **C(2)**; A(1); B(1) ... x3
5. **C(2)**; A(1); C(1); B(1) ... x3
6. **C(2)**; A(2); B(2) ... x3
7. **C(2)**; A(2); C(1); B(2) ... x3
8. **C(2)**; A(3); B(3) ... x3
9. **C(2)**; Λ(3); C(1); B(3) ... x3
10. **C(2)**; A(4); B(4) ... x3
11. **C(2)**; A(4); C(1); B(4) ... x3
12. **C(2)**; A(5); B(5) ... x3
13. **C(2)**; C(1); A(4); C(1); B(4); C(1) ... x3
14. **C(2)**; B(1); A(5); B(5); A(1) ... x3

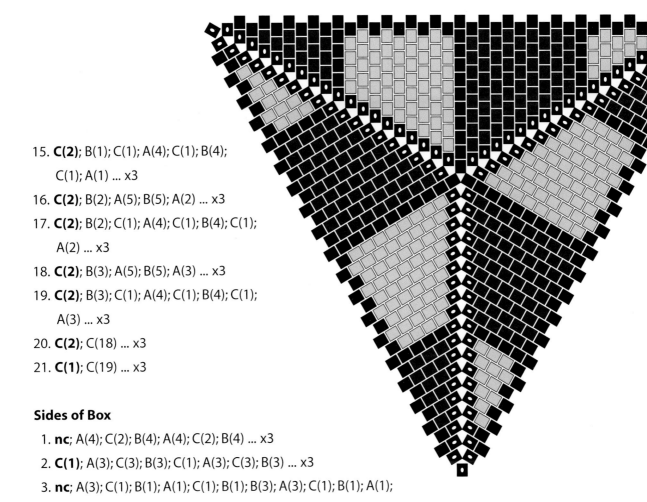

15. **C(2)**; B(1); C(1); A(4); C(1); B(4); C(1); A(1) ... x3

16. **C(2)**; B(2); A(5); B(5); A(2) ... x3

17. **C(2)**; B(2); C(1); A(4); C(1); B(4); C(1); A(2) ... x3

18. **C(2)**; B(3); A(5); B(5); A(3) ... x3

19. **C(2)**; B(3); C(1); A(4); C(1); B(4); C(1); A(3) ... x3

20. **C(2)**; C(18) ... x3

21. **C(1)**; C(19) ... x3

Sides of Box

1. **nc**; A(4); C(2); B(4); A(4); C(2); B(4) ... x3

2. **C(1)**; A(3); C(3); B(3); C(1); A(3); C(3); B(3) ... x3

3. **nc**; A(3); C(1); B(1); A(1); C(1); B(1); B(3); A(3); C(1); B(1); A(1); C(1); B(3) ... x3

4. **C(1)**; A(2); C(1); B(1); C(1); A(1); C(1); B(2); C(1); A(2); C(1); B(1); C(1); A(1); C(1); B(2) ... x3

5. **nc**; A(2); C(1); B(2); A(2); C(1); B(2); A(2); C(1); B(2); A(2); C(1); B(2) ... x3

6. **C(1)**; A(1); C(1); B(2); C(1); A(2); C(1); B(1); C(1); A(1); C(1); B(2); C(1); A(2); C(1); B(1) ... x3

7. **nc**; A(1); C(1); B(3); A(3); C(1); B(1); A(1); C(1); B(3); A(3); C(1); B(1) ... x3

8. **C(1)**; C(1); B(3); C(1); A(3); C(3); B(3); C(1); A(3); C(1) ... x3

9. **nc**; C(1); B(4); A(4); C(2); B(4); A(4); C(1) ... x3

10. **C(1);** B(4); C(1); A(4); C(1); B(4); C(1); A(4) ... x3

11. **nc**; C(20) ... x3

12. **C(1)**; C(19) ... x3

13. **nc**; C(1); A(4); B(4); C(2); A(4); B(4); C(1) ... x3

14. **C(1)**; C(1); A(3); C(1); B(3); C(3); A(3); C(1); B(3); C(1) ... x3

15. **nc**; B(1); C(1); A(3); B(3); C(1); A(1); B(1); C(1); A(3); B(3); C(1); A(1) ... x3

16. **C(1)**; B(1); C(1); A(2); C(1); B(2); C(1); A(1); C(1); B(1); C(1); A(2); C(1); B(2); C(1); A(1) ... x3

17. **nc**; B(2); C(1); A(2); B(2); C(1); A(2); B(2); C(1); A(2); B(2); C(1); A(2) ... x3

18. **C(1)**; B(2); C(1); A(1); C(1); B(1); C(1); A(2); C(1); B(2); C(1); A(1); C(1); B(1); C(1); A(2) ... x3

19. **nc**; B(3); C(1); A(1); B(1); C(1); A(3); B(3); C(1); A(1); B(1); C(1); A(3) ... x3

20. **C(1)**; B(3); C(3); A(3); C(1); B(3); C(3); A(3) ... x3

21. **nc**; B(4); C(2); A(4); B(4); C(2); A(4) ... x3

22. **C(1)**; B(4); C(1); A(4); C(1); B(4); C(1); A(4) ... x3

BEGIN HEM

23. **nc**; C(20) ... x3

24. **C(1)**; C(19) ... x3

Egypt

Finished Size: 2" wide
  x 1½" tall (5.1 x 3.8 cm)
  without finial or feet

A = Cream; Delica #157;
  507 beads (3 grams)

B = Yellow; Delica #205;
  546 beads (3 grams)

C = Mustard; Delica #272;
  576 beads (3 grams)

D = Brown; Delica #709;
  795 beads (3 grams)

Hem/Inner Wall = Any color;
  279 beads (2 grams)

| A | B | C | D |

Construction Techniques

For the Base: pages 15–16

For the Sides: pages 24–25

For the Flat Lid: pages 33–35

Base of Box

1. **C(1)** … x3
2. **C(2)** … x3
3. **C(2)**; B(1) … x3
4. **C(2)**; B(2) … x3
5. **D(2)**; B(1); A(1); B(1) … x3
6. **C(2)**; D(1); A(2); D(1) … x3
7. **B(2)**; C(1); D(1); A(1); D(1); C(1) … x3
8. **A(2)**; B(1); C(1); D(2); C(1); B(1) … x3
9. **D(2)**; A(1); B(1); D(3); B(1); A(1) … x3
10. **C(2)**; D(1); A(1); D(1); C(2); D(1); A(1); D(1) … x3
11. **B(2)**; C(1); D(2); C(3); D(2); C(1) … x3
12. **A(2)**; B(1); C(1); D(1); B(4); D(1); C(1); B(1) … x3
13. **D(2)**; A(1); B(1); C(1); D(1); B(3); D(1); C(1); B(1); A(1) … x3
14. **C(2)**; D(1); A(1); B(1); C(1); D(1); A(2); D(1); C(1); B(1); A(1); D(1) … x3
15. **B(2)**; C(1); D(1); A(1); B(1); C(1); D(1); A(1); D(1); C(1); B(1); A(1);
    D(1); C(1) … x3
16. **A(2)**; B(1); C(1); D(1); A(1); B(1); D(4); B(1); A(1); D(1); C(1); B(1) … x3
17. **D(2)**; A(1); B(1); D(2); A(1); D(1); C(1); D(1); C(1); D(1); A(1); D(2); B(1); A(1) … x3
18. **C(2)**; D(1); A(1); D(1); C(1); D(2); C(4); D(2); C(1); D(1); A(1); D(1) … x3

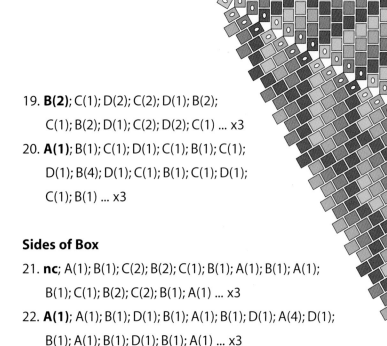

19. **B(2)**; C(1); D(2); C(2); D(1); B(2); C(1); B(2); D(1); C(2); D(2); C(1) ... x3

20. **A(1)**; B(1); C(1); D(1); C(1); B(1); C(1); D(1); B(4); D(1); C(1); B(1); C(1); D(1); C(1); B(1) ... x3

Sides of Box

21. **nc**; A(1); B(1); C(2); B(2); C(1); B(1); A(1); B(1); A(1); B(1); C(1); B(2); C(2); B(1); A(1) ... x3

22. **A(1)**; A(1); B(1); D(1); B(1); A(1); B(1); D(1); A(4); D(1); B(1); A(1); B(1); D(1); B(1); A(1) ... x3

23. **nc**; A(2); D(2); A(2); D(2); A(3); D(2); A(2); D(2); A(2) ... x3

24. **A(1)**; A(1); D(1); C(1); D(1); A(1); D(1); C(1); A(4); C(1); D(1); A(1); D(1); C(1); D(1); A(1) ... x3

25. **nc**; A(1); D(1); C(2); D(2); C(1); D(1); A(3); D(1); C(1); D(2); C(2); D(1); A(1) ... x3

26. **sc**; D(1); C(1); B(1); C(1); D(1); C(2); D(1); A(2); D(1); C(2); D(1); C(1); B(1); C(1); D(1) ... x3

27. **D(1)**; C(1); B(2); C(2); B(2); A(3); B(2); C(2); B(2); C(1) ... x3

28. **nc**; C(1); B(1); A(1); B(1); D(1); B(2); D(1); A(2); D(1); B(2); D(1); B(1); A(1); B(1); C(1) ... x3

29. **C(1)**; B(1); A(2); B(1); D(1); A(2); D(1); A(1); D(1); A(2); D(1); B(1); A(2); B(1) ... x3

30. **nc**; B(1); A(3); B(1); D(1); A(1); D(1); A(2); D(1); A(1); D(1); B(1); A(3); B(1) ... x3

31. **sc**; A(4); D(4); A(1); D(4); A(4) ... x3

32. **A(1)**; **A(3)**; D(1); C(1); D(1); C(1); **D(2)**; C(1); D(1); C(1); D(1); A(3) ... x3

33. **nc**; A(3); D(1); C(4); A(1); C(4); D(1); A(3) ... x3

34. **A(1)**; A(2); D(1); C(1); B(1); C(1); B(1); D(2); B(1); C(1); B(1); C(1); D(1); A(2) ... x3

35. **nc**; A(2); D(1); C(1); B(4); D(1); B(4); C(1); D(1); A(2) ... x3

36. **sc**; A(1); D(1); C(1); B(1); A(1); B(1); A(1); B(2); A(1); B(1); A(1); B(1); C(1); D(1); A(1) ... x3

37. **A(1)**; D(1); C(1); B(1); A(4); D(1); A(4); B(1); C(1); D(1) ... x3

38. **nc**; D(1); C(1); B(1); A(4); D(2); A(4); B(1); C(1); D(1) ... x3

39. **D(1)**; D(1); B(1); A(4); D(1); C(1); D(1); A(4); B(1); D(1) ... x3

40. **nc**; C(1); D(1); A(4); D(1); C(2); D(1); A(4); D(1); C(1) ... x3

41. **sc**; C(1); D(1); A(3); D(1); C(1); B(1); C(1); D(1); A(3); D(1); C(1) ... x3

42. **B(1)**; D(2); A(2); D(1); C(1); B(2); C(1); D(1); A(2); D(2) ... x3

43. **nc**; B(1); C(1); D(1); A(1); D(2); B(1); A(1); B(1); D(2); A(1); D(1); C(1); B(1) ... x3

44. **A(1)**; D(1); C(1); D(2); C(1); D(1); A(2); D(1); C(1); D(2); C(1); D(1) ... x3

45. **nc**; D(1); B(1); C(1); D(1); C(1); B(1); A(3); B(1); C(1); D(1); C(1); B(1); D(1) ... x3

46. **sc**; A(1); B(1); C(2); B(1); D(1); A(2); D(1); B(1); C(2); B(1); A(1) ... x3

47. **D(1)**; A(1); B(1); C(1); B(1); A(1); D(1); A(1); D(1); A(1); B(1); C(1); B(1); A(1) ... x3

48. **nc**; D(1); A(1); B(2); A(6); B(2); A(1); D(1) ... x3

49. **C(1)**; D(1); A(1); B(1); A(2); D(1); A(1); D(1);
    A(2); B(1); A(1); D(1) ... x3

50. **nc**; C(1); D(1); A(4); D(2); A(4); D(1);
    C(1) ... x3

51. **sc**; C(1); D(1); A(3); D(1); A(1); D(1);
    A(3); D(1); C(1) ... x3

52. **B(1)**; C(1); D(1); A(2); D(4); A(2);
    D(1); C(1) ... x3

53. **nc**; B(1); C(1); D(1); A(1); D(1);
    C(1); D(1); C(1); D(1); A(1);
    D(1); C(1); B(1) ... x3

54. **A(1)**; B(1); C(1); D(2); C(4);
    D(2); C(1); B(1) ... x3

55. **nc**; A(1); B(1); C(1); D(1); C(1); B(3); C(1); D(1); C(1); B(1); A(1) ... x3

56. **sc**; A(1); B(1); D(2); B(4); D(2); B(1); A(1) ... x3

57. **A(1)**; A(1); D(1); A(1); D(1); A(1); D(1); A(1); D(1); A(1); D(1); A(1) ... x3

58. **nc**; A(1); D(1); A(1); B(1); D(4); B(1); A(1); D(1); A(1) ... x3

59. **A(1)**; D(1); A(1); B(1); C(1); D(1); A(1); D(1); C(1); B(1); A(1); D(1) ... x3

BEGIN HEM

60. **nc**; D(1); A(1); B(1); C(1); D(1); A(2); D(1); C(1); B(1); A(1); D(1) ... x3

61. **D(1)**; A(1); B(1); C(1); D(1); B(3); D(1); C(1); B(1); A(1) ... x3

Flat Lid

1. **C(1)** ... x3

2. **C(2)** ... x3

3. **C(2)**; B(1) ... x3

4. **C(2)**; B(2) ... x3

5. **D(2)**; B(1); A(1); B(1) ... x3

6. **C(2)**; D(1); A(2); D(1) ... x3

7. **B(2)**; C(1); D(1); A(1); D(1); C(1) ... x3

8. **A(2)**; B(1); C(1); D(2); C(1); B(1) ... x3

9. **D(2)**; A(1); B(1); D(3); B(1); A(1) ... x3

10. **C(2)**; D(1); A(1); D(1); **C(2)**; D(1); A(1); D(1) ... x3

11. **B(2)**; C(1); D(2); C(3); D(2); C(1) ... x3

12. **A(2)**; B(1); C(1); D(1); B(4); D(1); C(1); B(1) ... x3

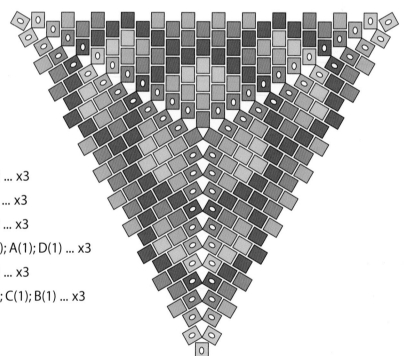

 # Red Knot

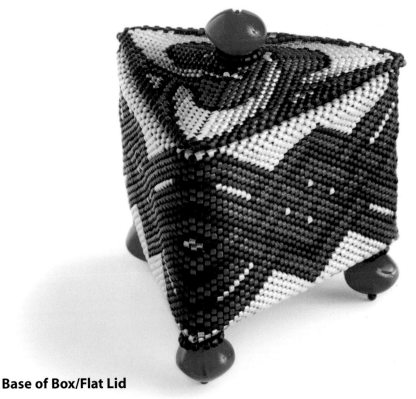

Finished Size: 2¼" wide
 x 1¾" tall (5.7 x 4.5 cm)
 without finial or feet

A = White; Delica #352;
 237 beads (2 grams)

B = Light Cream; Delica #353;
 492 beads (3 grams)

C = Medium Cream; Delica
 #205; 261 beads (2 grams)

D = Dark Cream; Delica #621;
 1,125 beads (6 grams)

E = Red; Delica #162;
 1,578 beads (8 grams)

F = Brown; Delica #769;
 1,638 beads (9 grams)

Hem/Inner Wall = Any color;
 852 beads (5 grams)

| A | B | C | D | E | F |

Construction Techniques

For the Base: pages 15–16

For the Sides: pages 24–25

For the Flat Lid: pages 33–35

Base of Box/Flat Lid

1. **E(1)** … x3
2. **E(2)** … x3
3. **E(2)**; E(1) … x3
4. **F(2)**; E(2) … x3
5. **C(2)**; E(3) … x3
6. **F(2)**; F(1); E(2); F(1) … x3
7. **E(2)**; D(1); F(1); E(1); F(1); C(1) … x3
8. **E(2)**; F(1); D(1); F(1); E(1); F(2) … x3
9. **E(2)**; E(1); F(1); D(1); F(1); E(1); F(1); E(1) … x3
10. **E(2)**; E(2); F(1); D(1); F(1); E(3) … x3

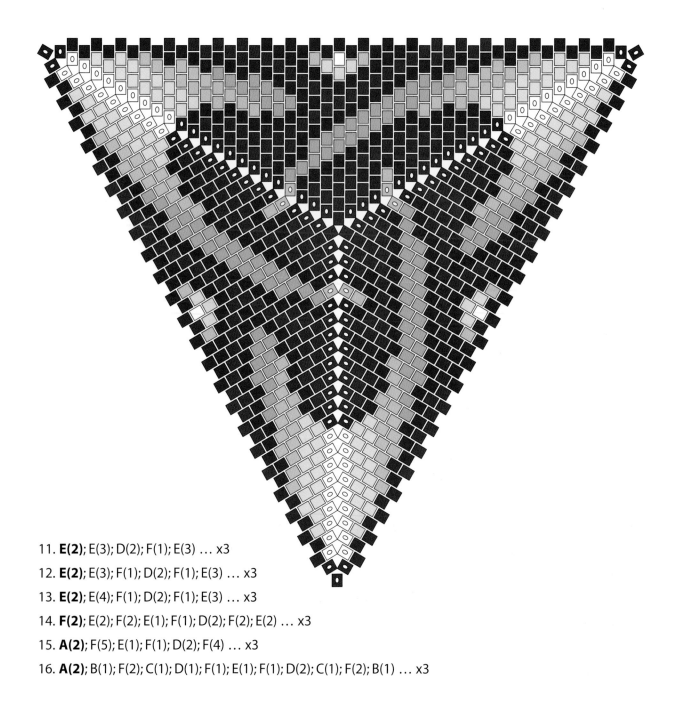

11. **E(2);** E(3); D(2); F(1); E(3) … x3

12. **E(2);** E(3); F(1); D(2); F(1); E(3) … x3

13. **E(2);** E(4); F(1); D(2); F(1); E(3) … x3

14. **F(2);** E(2); F(2); E(1); F(1); D(2); F(2); E(2) … x3

15. **A(2);** F(5); E(1); F(1); D(2); F(4) … x3

16. **A(2);** B(1); F(2); C(1); D(1); F(1); E(1); F(1); D(2); C(1); F(2); B(1) … x3

17. **A(2)**; B(2); C(2); D(2); F(1); E(1); F(1); D(2); C(2); B(2) … x3

18. **A(2)**; B(2); C(2); D(2); F(1); E(2); F(1); D(2); C(2); B(2) … x3

19. **A(2)**; B(2); C(2); D(2); F(1); E(1); F(1); E(1); F(1); D(2); C(2); B(2) … x3

20. **A(2)**; B(2); C(2); D(2); F(1); E(1); F(2); E(1); F(1); D(2); C(2); B(2) … x3

21. **A(2)**; B(2); C(2); D(1); F(2); E(1); F(1); B(1); F(1); E(1); F(2); D(1); C(2); B(2) … x3

22. **A(2)**; B(2); C(2); F(3); E(1); F(1); B(2); F(1); E(1); F(3); C(2); B(2) … x3

23. **A(2)**; B(2); C(1); F(3); E(2); F(1); C(1); A(1); C(1); F(1); E(2); F(3); C(1); B(2) … x3

24. **F(2)**; F(5); E(3); F(6); E(3); F(5) … x3

25. **F(1)**; F(4); E(4); F(7); E(4); F(4) … x3

Sides of Box

1. **nc**; D(3); C(3); B(3); A(6); B(3); C(3); D(3) … x3

2. **F(1)**; F(2); C(3); B(4); A(5); B(4); C(3); F(2) … x3

3. **nc**; F(3); C(3); B(3); A(6); B(3); C(3); F(3) … x3

4. **E(1)**; E(2); F(1); C(2); B(4); A(2); F(1); A(2); B(4); C(2); F(1); E(2) … x3

5. **nc**; E(3); F(1); C(2); B(3); A(2); F(2); A(2); B(3); C(2); F(1); E(3) … x3

6. **E(1)**; E(3); F(1); C(1); B(4); A(1); F(1); E(1); F(1); A(1); B(4); C(1); F(1); E(3) … x3

7. **nc**; E(4); F(1); C(1); B(3); A(1); F(1); E(2); F(1); A(1); B(3); C(1); F(1); E(4) … x3

8. **F(1)**; F(2); E(2); F(1); B(4); F(1); E(3); F(1); B(4); F(1); E(2); F(2) … x3

9. **nc**; F(3); E(2); F(1); B(3); F(1); **E(4)**; F(1); B(3); F(1); E(2); F(3) … x3

10. **E(1)**; F(1); D(1); F(1); E(2); F(1); B(2); F(1); E(2); F(1); E(2); F(1); B(2); F(1); E(2); F(1); D(1); F(1) … x3

11. **nc**; E(1); F(1); D(1); F(1); E(2); F(1); B(1); F(1); E(2); F(2); E(2); F(1); B(1); F(1); E(2); F(1); D(1); F(1); E(1) … x3

12. **E(1)**; E(1); F(1); C(1); F(1); E(2); F(2); E(2); F(3); E(2); F(2); E(2); F(1); C(1); F(1); E(1) … x3

13. **nc**; E(2); F(1); C(1); F(1); E(2); F(1); E(2); F(4); E(2); F(1); E(2); F(1); C(1); F(1); E(2) … x3

14. **F(1)**; E(2); F(1); C(1); F(1); E(2); F(1); E(1); F(2); E(1); F(2); E(2); F(1); E(1); F(1); C(1); F(1); E(2) … x3

15. **nc**; F(1); E(2); F(1); C(1); F(1); E(2); F(3); E(2); F(2); E(2); F(2); C(1); F(1); E(2); F(1) … x3

16. **F(1)**; F(1); E(2); F(1); C(1); F(1); E(2); F(2); E(3); F(2); E(2); F(1); C(1); F(1); E(2); F(1) … x3

17. **nc**; F(2); E(2); F(3); E(2); F(1); E(4); F(2); E(2); F(2); E(2); F(2) … x3

18. **E(1)**; F(2); E(2); F(1); E(1); F(1); E(1); F(1); E(2); F(1); E(1); F(1); E(1); F(1); E(2); F(1); E(2); F(2) … x3

19. **nc**; E(1); F(2); E(1); F(1); E(2); F(2); E(2); F(3); E(2); F(1); E(1); F(1); E(2); F(2); E(1) … x3

20. **E(1)**; E(1); F(3); E(2); F(2); E(2); F(1); A(1); F(1); E(2); F(3); E(2); F(2); E(1) … x3

21. **nc**; E(2); F(2); E(2); F(2); E(2); F(3); E(2); F(3); E(2); F(2); E(2) … x3

22. **F(1)**; E(2); F(1); E(2); F(2); E(2); F(1); E(1); F(1); E(2); F(1); E(1); F(1); E(2); F(2); E(2) … x3

23. **nc**; F(1); E(2); F(1); E(1); F(1); E(1); F(1); E(1); F(1); E(2); F(1); E(1); F(1); E(2); F(1); E(1); F(1); E(1); F(1); E(1); F(1) … x3

24. **D(1)**; F(1); E(2); F(2); E(2); F(3); E(2); F(3); E(2); F(2); E(2); F(2) … x3

25. **nc(1)**; D(1); F(1); E(2); F(2); E(2); F(1); A(1); F(1); E(2); F(1); A(1); F(1); E(2); F(2); E(2); F(1); D(1) … x3

26. **D(1)**; F(2); E(2); F(2); E(2); F(3); E(2); F(3); E(2); F(2); E(2); F(1) … x3

27. **nc**; F(1); E(1); F(1); E(1); F(1); E(1); F(1); E(2); F(1); E(1); F(1); E(2); F(1); E(1); F(1); E(1); F(1); E(1); F(1); E(2); F(1) … x3

28. **F(1)**; E(2); F(2); E(2); F(1); E(1); F(1); E(2); F(1); E(1); F(1); E(2); F(2); E(2); F(1); E(2) … x3

29. **nc**; E(2); F(2); E(2); F(3); E(2); F(3); E(2); F(2); E(2); F(2); E(2) … x3

30. **E(1)**; E(1); F(2); E(2); F(3); E(2); F(1); A(1); F(1); E(2); F(2); E(2); F(3); E(1) … x3

31. **nc**; E(1); F(2); E(2); F(1); E(1); F(1); E(2); F(3); E(2); F(2); E(2); F(1); E(1); F(2); E(1) … x3

32. **E(1)**; F(2); E(2); F(1); E(2); F(1); E(1); F(1); E(1); F(1); E(2); F(1); E(1); F(1); E(1); F(1); E(2); F(2) … x3

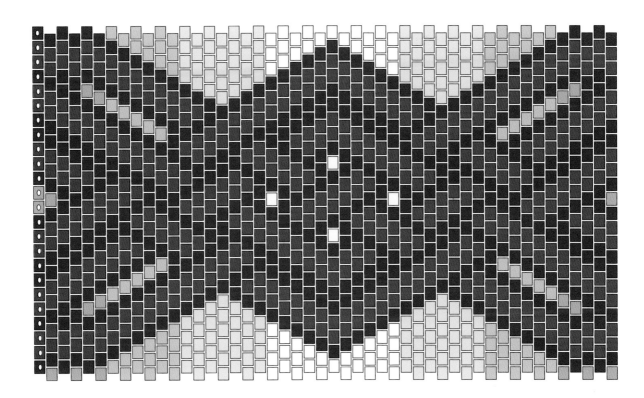

33. **nc**; F(2); E(2); F(2); E(2); F(2); E(4); F(1); E(2); F(3); E(2); F(2) … x3

34. **F(1)**; F(1); E(2); F(1); C(1); F(1); E(2); F(2); E(3); F(2); E(2); F(1); C(1); F(1); E(2); F(1) … x3

35. **nc**; F(1); E(2); F(1); C(1); F(2); E(2); F(2); E(2); F(3); E(2); F(1); C(1); F(1); E(2); F(1) … x3

36. **F(1)**; E(2); F(1); C(1); F(1); E(1); F(1); E(2); F(2); E(1); F(2); E(1); F(1); E(2); F(1); C(1);
    F(1); E(2) … x3

37. **nc**; E(2); F(1); C(1); F(1); E(2); F(1); E(2); F(4); E(2); F(1); E(2); F(1); C(1); F(1); E(2) … x3

38. **E(1)**; E(1); F(1); C(1); F(1); E(2); F(2); E(2); F(3); E(2); F(2); E(2); F(1); C(1); F(1); E(1) … x3

39. **nc**; E(1); F(1); D(1); F(1); E(2); F(1); B(1); F(1); E(2); F(2); E(2); F(1); B(1); F(1); E(2); F(1);
    D(1); F(1); E(1) … x3

40. **E(1)**; F(1); D(1); F(1); E(2); F(1); B(2); F(1); E(2); F(1); E(2); F(1); B(2); F(1); E(2); F(1); D(1); F(1) ... x3

41. **nc**; F(3); E(2); F(1); B(3); F(1); E(4); F(1); B(3); F(1); E(2); F(3) ... x3

42. **F(1)**; F(2); E(2); F(1); B(4); F(1); E(3); F(1); B(4); F(1); E(2); F(2) ... x3

43. **nc**; E(4); F(1); C(1); B(3); A(1); F(1); E(2); F(1); A(1); B(3); C(1); F(1); E(4) ... x3

44. **E(1)**; E(3); F(1); C(1); B(4); A(1); F(1); E(1); F(1); A(1); B(4); C(1); F(1); E(3) ... x3

45. **nc**; E(3); F(1); C(2); B(3); A(2); F(2); A(2); B(3); C(2); F(1); E(3) ... x3

46. **E(1)**; E(2); F(1); C(2); B(4); A(2); F(1); A(2); B(4); C(2); F(1); E(2) ... x3

BEGIN HEM

47. **nc**; F(3); C(3); B(3); A(6); B(3); C(3); F(3) ... x3

48. **F(1)**; F(2); C(3); B(4); A(5); B(4); C(3); F(2) ... x3

Patterns for
Hexagon
Boxes

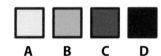 # Tuffet

Finished Size: 1³/₄" wide
x 1¹/₄" tall (4.5 x 3.2 cm)
without feet

A = White; Delica #157;
414 beads (3 grams)

B = Lavender; Delica #158;
480 beads (3 grams)

C = Purple; Delica #884;
462 beads (3 grams)

D = Black; Delica #310;
1,308 beads (7 grams)

Hem/Inner Wall = Any color;
288 beads (2 grams)

A	**B**	**C**	**D**

Construction Techniques

For the Base: pages 16–17

For the Sides: pages 24–26

Lid with Sides: pages 35–36

Base of Box

1. **nc**; C(1) ... x6

2. **B(1)** ... x6

3. **nc**; B(1) ... x6

4. **A(2)** ... x6

5. **A(1)**; D(1) ... x6

6. **nc**; D(2) ... x6

7. **D(2)**; C(1) ... x6

8. **D(1)**; C(2) ... x6

9. **nc**; C(1); B(1); C(1) ... x6

10. **D(2)**; B(2) ... x6

11. **C(1)**; B(1); A(1); B(1) ... x6

12. **nc**; D(1); A(2); D(1) ... x6

13. **C(2)**; D(1); A(1); D(1) ... x6

14. **B(1)**; C(1); D(2); C(1) ... x6

15. **nc**; B(1); D(3); B(1) ... x6

16. **A(2)**; D(1); C(2); D(1) ... x6

17. **A(1)**; B(1); C(1); B(1); C(1); B(1) ... x6

18. **nc**; D(2); B(2); D(2) ... x6

19. **D(2)**; D(1); B(1); A(1); B(1); D(1) ... x6

20. **D(1)**; C(1); D(1); A(2); D(1); C(1) ... x6

21. **nc**; C(2); D(1); A(1); D(1); C(2) ... x6

22. **C(2)**; B(1); C(1); D(2); C(1); B(1) ... x6

23. **C(1)**; B(2); C(1); D(1); C(1); B(2) ... x6

24. **nc**; B(1); A(1); B(1); D(2); B(1); A(1); B(1) ... x6

25. **D(2)**; A(2); D(1); C(1); D(1); A(2) ... x6

26. **D(1)**; D(1); A(1); D(1); C(2); D(1); A(1); D(1) ... x6

Sides of Box

27. **nc**; C(1); D(2); C(1); B(1); C(1); D(2); C(1) ... x6

28. **B(1)**; C(1); D(1); C(1); B(2); C(1); D(1); C(1) ... x6

29. **nc**; B(1); C(2); B(1); A(1); B(1); C(2); B(1) ... x6

30. **A(1)**; B(1); D(1); B(1); A(2); B(1); D(1); B(1) ... x6

31. **nc**; A(1); B(2); A(3); B(2); A(1) ... x6

32. **A(1)**; A(1); D(1); A(4); D(1); A(1) ... x6

33. **nc**; A(1); D(2); A(3); D(2); A(1) ... x6

34. **A(1)**; D(1); C(1); D(1); A(2); D(1); C(1); D(1) ... x6

35. **nc**; D(1); C(2); D(1); A(1); D(1); C(2); D(1) ... x6

36. **D(1)**; C(1); B(1); C(1); D(2); C(1); B(1); C(1) ... x6

37. **nc**; D(1); B(2); D(3); B(2); D(1) ... x6

38. **sc**; D(1); A(1); D(1); C(2); D(1); A(1); D(1) ... x6

39. **D(1)**; D(2); C(1); B(1); C(1); D(2) ... x6

40. **nc**; D(3); B(2); D(3) ... x6

41. **sc**; D(3); A(1); D(3) ... x6

42. **D(1)**; D(6) ... x6

43. **nc**; D(7) ... x6

44. **sc**; D(6) ... x6

45. **D(1)**; D(5) ... x6

46. **nc**; D(6) ... x6

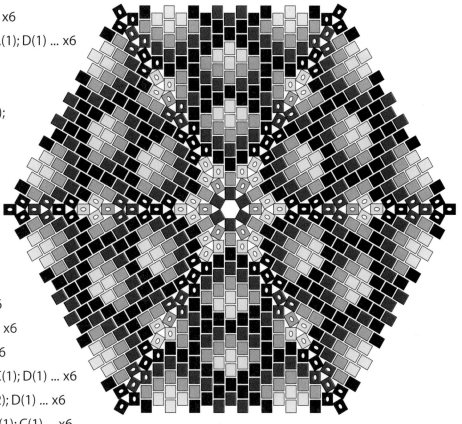

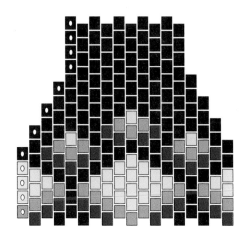

47. **sc**; D(5) ... x6

48. **D(1)**; D(4) ... x6

49. **nc**; D(5) ... x6

50. **D(1)**; D(4) ... x6

51. **nc**; D(5) ... x6

52. **D(1)**; D(4) ... x6

BEGIN HEM

53. **nc**; D(5) ... x6

54. **D(1)**; D(4) ... x6

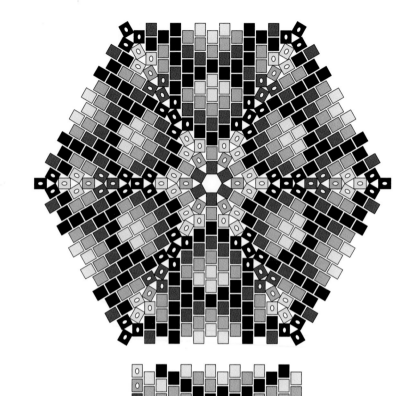

Lid with Sides

1. **nc**; C(1) ... x6

2. **B(1)** ... x6

3. **nc**; B(1) ... x6

4. **A(2)** ... x6

5. **A(1)**; D(1) ... x6

6. **nc**; D(2) ... x6

7. **D(2)**; C(1) ... x6

8. **D(1)**; C(2) ... x6

9. **nc**; C(1); B(1); C(1) ... x6

10. **D(2)**; B(2) ... x6

11. **C(1)**; B(1); A(1); B(1) ... x6

12. **nc**; D(1); A(2); D(1) ... x6

13. **C(2)**; D(1); A(1); D(1) ... x6

14. **B(1)**; C(1); D(2); C(1) ... x6

15. **nc**; B(1); D(3); B(1) ... x6

16. **A(2)**; D(1); C(2); D(1) ... x6

17. **A(1)**; B(1); C(1); B(1); C(1); B(1) ... x6

18. **nc**; D(2); B(2); D(2) ... x6

19. **D(2)**; D(1); B(1); A(1); B(1); D(1) ... x6

20. **D(1)**; C(1); D(1); A(2); D(1); C(1) ... x6

Sides of Lid

21. **nc**; C(2); D(1); A(1); D(1); C(2) ... x6

22. **C(1)**; B(2); D(2); B(2) ... x6

23. **nc**; B(2); D(3); B(2) ... x6

24. **B(1)**; A(1); D(1); B(2); D(1); A(1) ... x6

BEGIN HEM

25. **nc**; A(1); D(1); B(1); A(1); B(1); D(1); A(1) ... x6

26. **A(1)**; D(1); A(4); D(1) ... x6

 # Deco Pagoda

Finished Size: 2½" wide
x 2" tall (6.4 x 5.1 cm)
without finial or feet

A = White; Delica #200;
2,154 beads (11 grams)

B = Black; Delica #010;
2,706 beads (14 grams)

C = Red; Delica #723;
36 beads

D = Red; Size 8 seed beads
#408; 18 beads

Hem/Inner Wall = Any color;
342 beads (2 grams)

A	B	C	D

Construction Techniques

For the Base: pages 16–17

For the Sides: pages 24–26

For the Flat Lid: pages 33–35

This box is a little different in that it has a tiered structure. You begin each new tier (except the bottom one) with the same method used to make a hem, but you make decreases to complete the tier. The roofs are extensions of the top row of each tier. This structure becomes clear as you follow the word map.

Base of Box

1. **nc**; B(1) ... x6
2. **A(1)** ... x6
3. **nc**; B(1) ... x6
4. **B(2)** ... x6
5. **B(1)**; B(1) ... x6
6. **nc**; B(2) ... x6
7. **A(2)**; A(1) ... x6
8. **B(1)**; A(2) ... x6
9. **nc**; A(3) ... x6
10. **A(2)**; A(2) ... x6
11. **B(1)**; A(3) ... x6
12. **nc**; A(4) ... x6
13. **B(2)**; A(3) ... x6
14. **B(1)**; A(4) ... x6
15. **nc**; B(1); A(3); B(1) ... x6
16. **A(2)**; B(1); A(2); B(1) ... x6
17. **B(1)**; B(5) ... x6
18. **nc**; A(1); B(4); A(1) ... x6
19. **A(2)**; B(5) ... x6

20. **B(1)**; A(1); B(1); A(2); B(1); A(1) ... x6

21. **nc**; A(1); B(1); A(3); B(1); A(1) ... x6

22. **A(2)**; A(2); B(2); A(2) ... x6

23. **B(1)**; A(1); B(5); A(1) ... x6

24. **nc**; A(8) ... x6

25. **A(2)**; A(1); B(5); A(1) ... x6

26. **B(1)**; A(3); B(2); A(3) ... x6

27. **nc**; B(3); A(3); B(3) ... x6

28. **A(2)**; B(3); A(2); B(3) ... x6

29. **B(1)**; B(9) ... x6

Bottom Tier

1. **nc**; A(1); B(3); A(2); B(3); A(1) ... x6

2. **A(1)**; B(4); A(1); B(4) ... x6

3. **nc**; A(1); B(3); A(2); B(3); A(1) ... x6

4. **B(1)**; B(9) ... x6

5. **nc**; A(1); B(3); A(2); B(3); A(1) ... x6

6. **A(1)**; A(1); B(2); A(3); B(2); A(1) ... x6

7. **nc**; B(1); A(3); B(2); A(3); B(1) ... x6

8. **B(1);** B(1); A(2); B(3); A(2); B(1) ... x6

9. **nc**; B(10) ... x6

10. **B(1)**; B(1); A(2); B(3); A(2); B(1) ... x6

11. **nc**; B(2); A(1); B(4); A(1); B(2) ... x6

12. **B(1)**; B(1); A(2); B(3); A(2); B(1) ... x6

13. **nc**; B(10) ... x6

14. **B(1);** B(1); A(2); B(3); A(2); B(1) ... x6

15. **nc**; B(1); A(3); B(2); A(3); B(1) ... x6

16. **A(1)**; A(1); B(2); A(3); B(2); A(1) ... x6

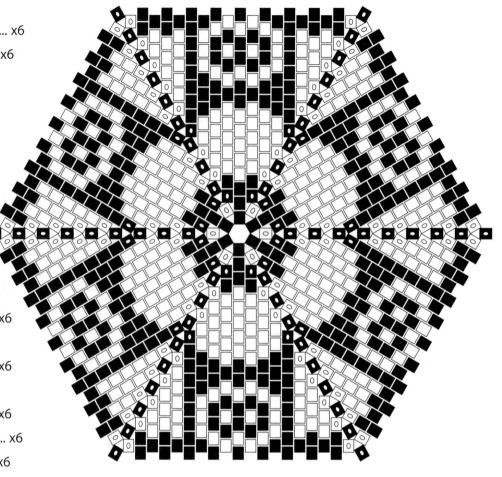

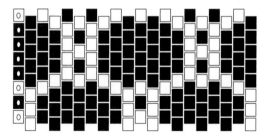

Bottom Tier

Middle Tier

Bead row 1 exactly as you would bead the first hem row. The skipped corner is considered an "**sc.**"

  1. **sc**; A(9) ... x6

The next five rows use Steps 2, 3, 1, 2, and 3 of a hexagon box decrease cycle (page 26).

You then resume tubular peyote stitch.

  2. **A(1)**; A(1); B(1); A(4); B(1); A(1) ... x6

  3. **nc**; A(1); B(1); A(2); B(1); A(2); B(1); A(1) ... x6

  4. **sc**; B(1); A(2); B(2); A(2); B(1) ... x6

  5. **B(1)**; B(1); A(1); B(1); C(1); B(1); A(1); B(1) ... x6

  6. **nc**; A(1); B(6); A(1) ... x6

  7. **A(1)**; A(1); B(1); A(1); B(1); A(1); B(1); A(1) ... x6

  8. **nc**; A(2); B(1); A(2); B(1); A(2) ... x6

  9. **B(1)**; A(2); B(1); A(1); B(1); A(2) ... x6

10. **nc**; B(1); A(2); B(2); A(2); B(1) ... x6

11. **C(1)**; B(1); A(2); B(1); A(2); B(1) ... x6

12. **nc**; B(2); A(1); B(2); A(1); B(2) ... x6

13. **B(1)**; A(1); B(2); C(1); B(2); A(1) ... x6

14. **nc**; A(2); B(4); A(2) ... x6

15. **A(1)**; A(1); B(1); A(1); B(1); A(1); B(1); A(1) ... x6

16. **nc**; A(1); B(1); A(4); B(1); A(1) ... x6

17. **A(1)**; B(1); A(5); B(1) ... x6

18. **nc**; B(1); A(6); B(1) ... x6

19. **B(1)**; A(7) ... x6

Middle Tier

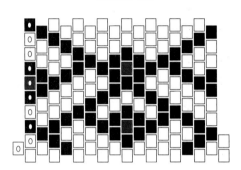

Top Tier

Bead row 1 exactly as you would bead the first hem row.

The skipped corner is considered an "**sc.**"

  1. **sc**; B(7) ... x6

Top Tier

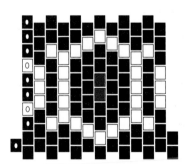

The next five rows use Steps 2, 3, 1, 2, and 3 of a hexagon box decrease cycle (pages 26–27). You then resume tubular peyote stitch.

2. **B(1)**; B(6) ... x6

3. **nc**; B(3); A(1); B(3) ... x6

4. **sc**; B(2); A(2); B(2) ... x6

5. **B(1)**; A(2); B(1); A(2) ... x6

6. **nc**; B(1); A(1); B(2) ... x6

7. **A(1)**; B(5) ... x6

8. **nc**; A(2); B(2); A(2) ... x6

9. **B(1)**; B(2); C(1); B(2) ... x6

10. **nc**; A(2); B(2); A(2) ... x6

11. **B(1)**; B(2); C(1); B(2) ... x6

12. **nc**; A(2); B(2); A(2) ... x6

13. **A(1)**; B(5) ... x6

14. **nc**; B(1); A(1); B(2); A(1); B(1) ... x6

15. **B(1)**; A(2); B(1); A(2) ... x6

16. **nc**; B(2); A(2); B(2) ... x6

17. **B(1)**; B(2); A(1); B(2) ... x6

BEGIN HEM

18. **nc**; B(6) ... x6

19. **B(1)**; B(5) ... x6

You will now add first the middle roof and then the bottom roof. Begin a new thread, and weave through the appropriate tier until your needle exits the last (top) row of the tier. (This row is indicated

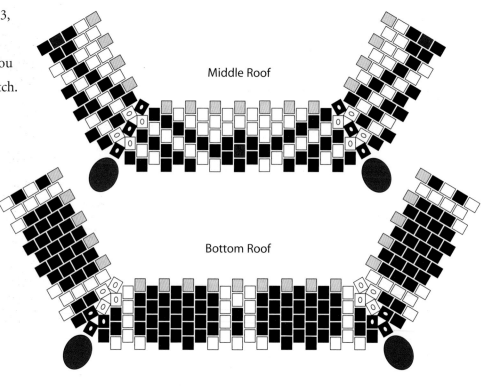

Middle Roof

Bottom Roof

by the grey beads in the diagram.) You will then add one row without increasing (the corner will be a down bead) and then perform two and one-half hexagon-box increase cycles.

Begin the third cycle in the usual way, but in the second step of the increase—where you would usually add two corner beads—add one "D" bead. This row will be the final row of the roof. Read the graph from the top row downward. (The graph shows a full roof side with partial sides adjoining. The partial sides are for reference only.)

Middle Roof

1. **nc**; B(1); A(6); B(1) … x6

2. **A(2)**; B(1); A(5); B(1) … x6

3. **B(1)**; A(1); B(1); A(4); B(1); A(1) … x6

4. **nc**; B(1); A(1); B(1); A(1); B(1); A(1); B(1); A(1); B(1) … x6

5. **A(2)**; B(1); A(1); B(4); A(1); B(1) … x6

6. **B(1)**; A(1); B(1); A(1); B(1); C(1); B(1); A(1); B(1); A(1) … x6

7. **nc**; B(1); A(1); B(1); A(1); B(2); A(1); B(1); A(1); B(1) … x6

8. **D(1)**; B(3); A(1); B(1); A(1); B(3) … x6

Bottom Roof

1. **nc**; A(1); B(3); A(2); B(3); A(1) … x6

2. **A(2)**; B(9) … x6

3. **B(1)**; A(1); B(3); A(2); B(3); A(1) … x6

4. **nc**; B(5); A(1); B(5) … x6

5. **B(2)**; A(1); B(3); A(2); B(3); A(1) … x6

6. **B(1)**; B(11) … x6

7. **nc**; B(1); A(1); B(3); A(2); B(3); A(1); B(1) … x6

8. **D(1)**; A(2); B(2); A(3); B(2); A(2) … x6

Flat Lid

1. **nc**; B(1) … x6

2. **A(1)** … x6

3. **nc**; B(1) … x6

4. **B(2)** … x6

5. **B(1)**; B(1) … x6

6. **nc**; B(2) … x6

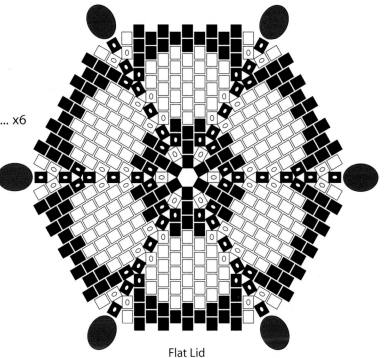

Flat Lid

7. **A(2)**; A(1) … x6

8. **B(1)**; A(2) … x6

9. **nc**; A(3) … x6

10. **A(2)**; A(2) … x6

11. **B(1)**; A(3) … x6

12. **nc**; A(4) … x6

13. **B(2)**; A(3) … x6

14. **B(1)**; A(4) … x6

15. **nc**; B(1); A(3); B(1) … x6

16. **A(2)**; B(1); A(2); B(1) … x6

17. **B(1)**; B(5) … x6

18. **nc**; A(1); B(4); A(1) … x6

19. **D(1)**; B(5) … x6

 # New School

Finished Size: 3" wide x
  2¼" tall (7.6 x 5.7 cm)
  without finial or feet

A = Dark Cream; Delica #907;
  1,494 beads (8 grams)

B = Yellow; Delica #124;
  418 beads (3 grams)

C = Pale Pink; Delica #728;
  96 beads (1 gram)

D = Turquoise; Delica #217;
  284 beads (2 grams)

E = Green; Delica #859;
  776 beads (4 grams)

F = Purple; Delica #884;
  584 beads (3 grams)

G = Black; Delica #10;
  3,238 beads (17 grams)

Hem/Inner Wall = Any color;
  684 beads (4 grams)

A   B   C   D   E   F   G

Construction Techniques

For the Base: pages 16–17

For the Sides: pages 24–26

For the Flat Lid: pages 33–35

Base of Box

Flat strip (indicated on the graph by ovals inside of squares)

  1 and 2. G(1); D(1); G(2); E(1); G(2); D(1); G(2); E(1); G(2); D(1); G(2); E(1);
    G(2); D(1); G(1) ... x1

  3. D(2); G(1); D(2); G(1); D(2); G(1); D(2) ... x1

  4. D(1); G(2); D(1); G(2); D(1); G(2); D(1) ... x1

  5. G(2); E(1); G(2); E(1); G(2); E(1); G(2) ... x1

Add end beads.

  6. G(1); E(2); G(1); E(2); G(1); E(2); G(1); **G(3)** (end beads) ... x2

  7. G(2); E(1); G(2); E(1); G(2); E(1); G(2); G(1) (between end beads);
    G(1) (between end beads) ... x2

  8. F(1); G(2); F(1); G(2); F(1); G(2); F(1); **G(2)**; **F(2)**; **G(2)** ... x2

Begin hexagon increase cycles. From this point on, read the word map
as usual, beginning with corner beads. The long sides will be first.

9. **G(1)**; F(2); G(1); F(2); G(1); F(2); G(1); F(2); G(1); F(1); **F(1)**; F(1) ... x2

10. **nc**; G(1); F(1); G(2); F(1); G(2); F(1); G(4); **nc**; G(1); F(1); **nc**; F(1); G(1) ... x2

11. **C(2);** G(5); C(1); G(2); E(1); G(2); **C(2)**; G(1); **F(2)**; G(1) ... x2

12. **C(1)**; C(1); G(2); B(1); G(1); C(2); G(1); E(1); G(1); A(1); G(1); **C(1)**; C(1); G(1); **F(1)**; G(2) ... x2

13. **nc**; C(1); G(2); B(2); G(1); C(1); G(3); A(1); G(2); **nc**; C(1); G(2); **nc**; G(3) ... x2

14. **G(2)**; G(1); E(1); B(3); G(2); D(1); G(1); A(1); G(1); E(1); **G(2)**; G(1); E(1); **G(2)**; G(1); E(1) ... x2

15. **G(1)**; G(1); E(1); G(1); B(3); G(1); D(1); G(1); A(1); G(1); E(1); G(1); **G(1)**; G(1); E(1); G(1); **G(1)**; G(1); E(1); G(1) ... x2

16. **nc**; G(1); E(2); G(1); B(3); G(2); A(1); G(1); E(2); G(1); **nc**; G(1); E(2); G(1); **nc**; G(1); E(2); G(1) ... x2

17. **G(2)**; E(3); G(1); B(2); G(2); A(1); G(1); E(3); **G(2)**; E(3); **G(2)**; E(3) ...x2

18. **E(1)**; E(4); G(1); B(1); G(2); A(1); G(1); E(4); **E(1)**; E(4); **E(1)**; E(4) ... x2

19. **nc**; E(5); G(2); A(2); G(1); E(5); **nc;** E(5); **nc**; E(5) ... x2

20. **E(2)**; E(5); G(1); A(2); G(1); E(5); **E(2)**; E(4); **E(2)**; E(4) ... x2

21. **E(1)**; E(6); A(3); E(6); **E(1)**; E(5); **E(1)**; E(5) ... x2

22. **nc**; E(6); G(1); A(2); G(1); E(6); **nc**; E(6); **nc**; E(6) ... x2

23. **G(2)**; E(5); G(2); A(2); G(1); E(5); **G(2)**; E(5); **G(2)**; E(5) ... x2

24. **B(1)**; G(1); E(4); G(1); B(1); G(2); A(1); G(1); E(4); G(1); **B(1)**; G(1); E(4); G(1); **B(1)**; G(1); E(4); G(1) ... x2

25. **nc**; A(1); G(1); E(3); G(1); B(2); G(2); A(1); G(1); E(3); G(1); B(1); **nc**; A(1); G(1); E(3); G(1); B(1); **nc**; A(1); G(1); E(3); G(1); B(1) ...x2

26. **B/G**; A(1); G(1); E(2); G(1); B(3); F(1); G(1); A(1); G(1); E(2); G(1); B(1); **B/G**; A(1); G(1); E(2); G(1); B(1); **B/G**; A(1); G(1); E(2); G(1); B(1) ... x2

27. **G(1)**; G(1); A(1); G(1); E(1); G(1); B(3); G(1); F(1); G(1); A(1); G(1); E(1); G(1); B(2); **G(1)**; G(1); A(1); G(1); E(1); G(1); B(2); **G(1)**; G(1); A(1); G(1); E(1); G(1); B(2) ... x2

28. **nc**; F(1); G(1); A(1); G(1); E(1); B(3); G(1); F(2); G(1); A(1); G(1); E(1); B(3); **nc**; F(1); G(1); A(1); G(1); E(1); B(3); **nc**; F(1); G(1); A(1); G(1); E(1); B(3) ... x2

29. **G/F**; F(1); G(1); A(1); G(2); B(2); G(1); F(3); G(1); A(1); G(2); B(2); **G/F**; F(1); G(1); A(1); G(2); B(2); **G/F**; F(1); G(1); A(1); G(2); B(2) ... x2

30. **F(1)**; F(2); G(1); A(1); G(2); B(1); G(1); F(4); G(1); A(1); G(2); B(1); G(1); **F(1)**; F(2); G(1); A(1); G(2); B(1); G(1); **F(1)**; F(2); G(1); A(1); G(2); B(1); G(1) ... x2

31. **nc**; F(3); G(1); A(2); G(2); F(5); G(1); A(2); G(2); F(1); **nc**; F(3); G(1); A(2); G(2); F(1); **nc**; F(3); G(1); A(2); G(2); F(1) ... x2

32. **F(2)**; F(3); G(1); A(2); G(1); F(6); G(1); A(2); G(1); F(1); **F(2)**; F(3); G(1); A(2); G(1); F(1); **F(2)**; F(3); G(1); A(2); G(1); F(1) ... x2

33. **F(1)**; F(4); A(3); F(7); A(3); F(2); **F(1)**; F(4); A(3); F(2); **F(1)**; F(4); A(3); F(2) ... x2

Sides of Box

Everyone beads differently, depending sometimes on which hand is dominant or on natural tendency. Some people will prefer to bead the base in a clockwise direction, and others will bead counterclockwise. Because the pattern is read clockwise, the side of the beadwork that is facing you may or may not be a mirror image of the graphed pattern.

Similarly, some beaders will naturally work the sides of the box away from their bodies (with the underside of the box facing toward them). Others will work the sides of the box toward their bodies (with the inside of the box facing them). Work whichever way is most comfortable for you, but, after adding the first few beads for the sides, look closely at your beadwork. The dark lines of the pattern should align from the base to the sides. If they do not, remove the beads from this row, and turn the base so that the opposite side of the box faces you. You will need to weave through a few beads to reorient the needle so that it is traveling in the right direction. Rework the row so that the pattern lines on the side and the base align.

1. **nc**; F(2); G(1); A(2); G(1); F(6); G(1); A(2); G(1); F(4); **nc**; F(2); G(1); A(2); G(1); F(4); **nc**; F(2); G(1); A(2); G(1); F(4) ... x2

2. **F(1)**; F(1); G(2); A(2); G(1); F(5); G(2); A(2); G(1); F(3); **F(1)**; F(1); G(2); A(2); G(1); F(3); **F(1)**; F(1); G(2); A(2); G(1); F(3) ... x2

3. **nc**; F(1); G(1); B(1); G(2); A(1); G(1); F(4); G(1); B(1); G(2); A(1); G(1); F(3); **nc**; F(1); G(1); B(1); G(2); A(1); G(1); F(3); **nc**; F(1); G(1); B(1); G(2); A(1); G(1); F(3) ... x2

4. **F(1)**; G(2); B(1); G(2); A(1); G(1); F(3); G(2); B(1); G(2); A(2); G(1); F(2); **F(1)**; G(2); B(1); G(2); A(1); G(1); F(2); **F(1)**; G(2); B(1); G(2); A(1); G(1); F(2) ... x2

5. **nc**; G(1); B(1); G(1); B(1); E(1); G(1); A(1); G(1); F(2); G(1); B(1); G(1); B(1); E(1); G(1); A(1); G(1); F(2); **nc**; G(1); B(1); G(1); B(1); E(1); G(1); A(1); G(1); F(2); **nc**; G(1); B(1); G(1); B(1); E(1); G(1); A(1); G(1); F(2) ... x2

6. **G(1)**; G(1); B(1); G(4); A(1); G(1); F(1); G(2); B(1); G(4); A(1); G(1); F(1); **G(1)**; G(1); B(1); G(4); A(1); G(1); F(1); **G(1)**; G(1); B(1); G(4); A(1); G(1); F(1) ... x2

7. **nc**; B(1); G(1); B(1); G(4); A(1); G(1); F(1); B(1); G(1); B(1); G(4); A(1); G(1); F(1); **nc**; B(1); G(1); B(1); G(4); A(1); G(1); F(1); **nc**; B(1); G(1); B(1); G(4); A(1); G(1); F(1) ... x2

8. **G(1)**; B(1); G(3); D(1); G(2); A(1); G(2); B(1); G(3); D(1); G(2); A(1); G(1); **G(1)**; B(1); G(3); D(1); G(2); A(1); G(1); **G(1)**; B(1); G(3); D(1); G(2); A(1); G(1) ... x2

9. **nc**; G(1); B(1); G(1); E(1); D(2); E(1); G(1); A(1); G(2); B(1); G(1); E(1); D(2); E(1); G(1); A(1); G(1); **nc**; G(1); B(1); G(1); E(1); D(2); E(1); G(1); A(1); G(1); **nc**; G(1); B(1); G(1); E(1); D(2); E(1); G(1); A(1); G(1) ... x2

10. **A(1)**; G(4); D(1); G(1); E(1); G(1); A(2); G(4); D(1); G(1); E(1); G(1); A(1); **A(1)**; G(4); D(1); G(1); E(1); G(1); A(1); **A(1)**; G(4); D(1); G(1); E(1); G(1) ... x2

11. **nc**; A(1); G(1); D(1); G(3); E(2); G(1); A(2); G(1); D(1); G(3); E(2); G(1); A(1); **nc**; A(1); G(1); D(1); G(3); E(2); G(1); A(1); **nc**; A(1); G(1); D(1); G(3); E(2); G(1); A(1) ... x2

12. **A(1)**; A(1); D(2); E(1); G(1); E(1); G(1); E(1); A(3); D(2); E(1); G(1); E(1); G(1); E(1); A(1); **A(1)**; A(1); D(2); E(1); G(1); E(1); G(1); E(1); A(1); **A(1)**; A(1); D(2); E(1); G(1); E(1); G(1); E(1); A(1) ... x2

13. **nc**; A(1); G(1); D(1); G(3); E(2); G(1); A(2); G(1); D(1); G(3); E(2); G(1); A(1); **nc**; A(1); G(1); D(1); G(3); E(2); G(1); A(1); **nc**; A(1); G(1); D(1); G(3); E(2); G(1); A(1) ... x2

14. **A(1)**; G(4); D(1); G(1); E(1); G(1); A(2); G(4); D(1); G(1); E(1); G(1); A(1); **A(1)**; G(4); D(1); G(1); E(1); G(1); A(1); **A(1)**; G(4); D(1); G(1); E(1); G(1); A(1) ... x2

15. **nc**; G(1); B(1); G(1); E(1); D(2); E(1); G(1); A(1); G(2);
    B(1); G(1); E(1); D(2); E(1); G(1); A(1); G(1); **nc**; G(1);
    B(1); G(1); E(1); D(2); E(1); G(1); A(1); G(1); **nc**; G(1);
    B(1); G(1); E(1); D(2); E(1); G(1); A(1); G(1) ... x2

16. **G(1)**; B(1); G(3); D(1); G(2); A(1); G(2); B(1); G(3);
    D(1); G(2); A(1); G(1); **G(1)**; B(1); G(3); D(1); G(2);
    A(1); G(1); **G(1)**; B(1); G(3); D(1); G(2); A(1);
    G(1) ... x2

17. **nc**; B(1); G(1); B(1); G(4); A(1); G(1); C(1); B(1); G(1);
    B(1); G(4); A(1); G(1); C(1); **nc**; B(1); G(1); B(1);
    G(4); A(1); G(1); C(1); **nc**; B(1); G(1); B(1); G(4);
    A(1); G(1); C(1) ... x2

18. **G(1)**; G(1); B(1); G(4); A(1); G(4); B(1); G(4); A(1);
    G(2); **G(1)**; G(1); B(1); G(4); A(1); G(2); **G(1)**; G(1);
    B(1); G(4); A(1); G(2) ... x2

19. **nc**; G(1); B(1); G(1); B(1); E(1); G(1); A(1); G(4); B(1);
    G(1); B(1); E(1); G(1); A(1); G(3); **nc**; G(1); B(1);
    G(1); B(1); E(1); G(1); A(1); G(3); **nc**; G(1); B(1);
    G(1); B(1); E(1); G(1); A(1); G(3) ... x2

20. **G(1)**; G(2); B(1); G(2); A(1); G(2); F(1); G(3); B(1);
    G(2); A(1); G(2); F(1); **G(1)**; G(2); B(1); G(2); A(1);
    G(2); F(1); **G(1)**; G(2); B(1); G(2); A(1); G(2); F(1) ... x2

21. **nc**; C(1); G(1); B(1); G(2); A(1); G(1); C(1); F(2);
    C(1); G(1); B(1); G(2); A(1); G(1); C(1); F(2); **nc**;
    C(1); G(1); B(1); G(2); A(1); G(1); C(1); F(2); **nc**;
    C(1); G(1); B(1); G(2); A(1); G(1); C(1); F(2) ... x2

22. **G(1)**; G(3); A(2); G(1); C(1); G(1); F(1); G(4);
    A(2); G(1); C(1); G(1); F(1); **G(1)**; G(3); A(2); G(1);

C(1); G(1); F(1); **G(1)**; G(3); A(2); G(1); C(1);
    G(1); F(1) ... x2

23. **nc**; G(1); F(1); G(1); A(2); G(1); C(2); G(3); F(1);
    G(1); A(2); G(1); C(2); G(2); **nc**; G(1); F(1); G(1);
    A(2); G(1); C(2); G(2); **nc**; G(1); F(1); G(1); A(2);
    G(1); C(2); G(2) ... x2

24. **C(1)**; F(2); A(3); C(1); G(1); C(1); G(1); C(1); F(2); A(3);
    C(1); G(1); C(1); G(1); **C(1)**; F(2); A(3); C(1); G(1); C(1);
    G(1); **C(1)**; F(2); A(3); C(1); G(1); C(1); G(1) ... x2

25. **nc**; G(1); F(1); G(1); A(2); G(1); C(2); G(3); F(1);
    G(1); A(2); G(1); C(2); G(2); **nc**; G(1); F(1); G(1);
    A(2); G(1); C(2); G(2); **nc**; G(1); F(1); G(1); A(2);
    G(1); C(2); G(2) ... x2

26. **G(1)**; G(3); A(2); G(1); C(1); G(1); F(1); G(4); A(2);
    G(1); C(1); G(1); F(1); **G(1)**; G(3); A(2); G(1); C(1);
    G(1); F(1); **G(1)**; G(3); A(2); G(1); C(1); G(1);
    F(1) ... x2

27. **nc**; C(1); G(1); B(1); G(2); A(1); G(1); C(1); F(2);
    C(1); G(1); B(1); G(2); A(1); G(1); C(1); F(2); **nc**;
    C(1); G(1); B(1); G(2); A(1); G(1); C(1); F(2); **nc**;
    C(1); G(1); B(1); G(2); A(1); G(1); C(1); F(2) ... x2

28. **G(1)**; G(2); B(1); G(2); A(1); G(2); F(1); G(3); B(1);
    G(2); A(1); G(2); F(1); **G(1)**; G(2); B(1); G(2); A(1);
    G(2); F(1); **G(1)**; G(2); B(1); G(2); A(1); G(2); F(1) ... x2

29. **nc**; G(1); B(1); G(1); B(1); E(1); G(1); A(1); G(4); B(1);
    G(1); B(1); E(1); G(1); A(1); G(3); **nc**; G(1); B(1);
    G(1); B(1); E(1); G(1); A(1); G(3); **nc**; G(1); B(1);
    G(1); B(1); E(1); G(1); A(1); G(3) ... x2

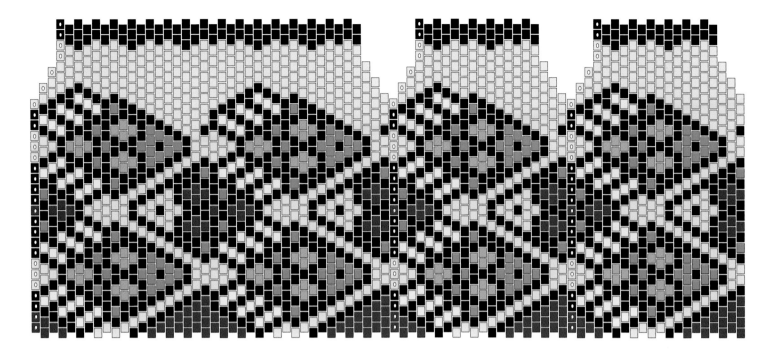

30. **G(1)**; G(1); B(1); G(4); A(1); G(4); B(1); G(4); A(1); G(2); **G(1)**; G(1); B(1); G(4); A(1); G(2); **G(1)**; G(1); B(1); G(4); A(1); G(2) ... x2

31. **nc**; B(1); G(1); B(1); G(4); A(1); G(1); C(1); B(1); G(1); B(1); G(4); A(1); G(1); C(1); **nc**; B(1); G(1); B(1); G(4); A(1); G(1); C(1); **nc**; B(1); G(1); B(1); G(4); A(1); G(1); C(1) ... x2

32. **G(1)**; B(1); G(3); D(1); G(2); A(1); G(2); B(1); G(3); D(1); G(2); A(1); G(1); **G(1)**; B(1); G(3); D(1); G(2); A(1); G(1); **G(1)**; B(1); G(3); D(1); G(2); A(1); G(1) ... x2

33. **nc**; G(1); B(1); G(1); E(1); D(2); E(1); G(1); A(1); G(2); B(1); G(1); E(1); D(2); E(1); G(1); A(1); G(1); **nc**; G(1); B(1); G(1); E(1); D(2); E(1); G(1); A(1); G(1); **nc**; G(1); B(1); G(1); E(1); D(2); E(1); G(1); A(1); G(1) ... x2

34. **A(1)**; G(4); D(1); G(1); E(1); G(1); A(2); G(4); D(1); G(1); E(1); G(1); A(1); **A(1)**; G(4); D(1); G(1); E(1); G(1); A(1); **A(1)**; G(4); D(1); G(1); E(1); G(1); A(1) ... x2

35. **nc**; A(1); G(1); D(1); G(3); E(2); G(1); A(2); G(1); D(1); G(3); E(2); G(1); A(1); **nc**; A(1); G(1); D(1); G(3); E(2); G(1); A(1); **nc**; A(1); G(1); D(1); G(3); E(2); G(1); A(1) ... x2

36. **A(1)**; A(1); D(2); E(1); G(1); E(1); G(1); E(1); A(3); D(2); E(1); G(1); E(1); G(1); E(1); A(1); **A(1)**; A(1); D(2); E(1); G(1); E(1); G(1); E(1); A(1); **A(1)**; A(1); D(2); E(1); G(1); E(1); G(1); E(1); A(1) ... x2

37. **nc**; A(1); G(1); D(1); G(3); E(2); G(1); A(2); G(1); D(1); G(3); E(2); G(1); A(1); **nc**; A(1); G(1); D(1); G(3); E(2); G(1); A(1); **nc**; A(1); G(1); D(1); G(3); E(2); G(1); A(1) ... x2

38. **A(1)**; G(4); D(1); G(1); E(1); G(1); A(2); G(4); D(1); G(1); E(1); G(1); A(1); **A(1)**; G(4); D(1); G(1); E(1); G(1); A(1); **A(1)**; G(4); D(1); G(1); E(1); G(1) ... x2

39. **nc**; G(1); B(1); G(1); E(1); D(2); E(1); G(1); A(1); G(2); B(1); G(1); E(1); D(2); E(1); G(1); A(1); G(1); **nc**; G(1); B(1); G(1); E(1); D(2); E(1); G(1); A(1); G(1); **nc**; G(1); B(1); G(1); E(1); D(2); E(1); G(1); A(1); G(1) ... x2

40. **G(1)**; B(1); G(3); D(1); G(2); A(2); G(1); B(1); G(3); D(1); G(2); A(2); **G(1)**; B(1); G(3); D(1); G(2); A(2); **G(1)**; B(1); G(3); D(1); G(2); A(2) ... x2

41. **nc**; B(1); G(1); B(1); G(4); A(3); B(1); G(1); B(1); G(4); A(3); **nc**; B(1); G(1); B(1); G(4); A(3); **nc**; B(1); G(1); B(1); G(4); A(3) ... x2

42. **G(1)**; G(1); B(1); G(4); A(3); G(2); B(1); G(4); A(3); **G(1)**; G(1); B(1); G(4); A(3); **G(1)**; G(1); B(1); G(4); A(3) ... x2

43. **nc**; G(1); B(1); G(1); B(1); E(1); G(1); A(4); G(1); B(1); G(1); B(1); E(1); G(1); A(4); **nc**; G(1); B(1); G(1); B(1); E(1); G(1); A(4); **nc**; G(1); B(1); G(1); B(1); E(1); G(1); A(4) ... x2

44. **A(1)**; G(2); B(1); G(2); A(5); G(2); B(1); G(2); A(4); **A(1)**; G(2); B(1); G(2); A(4); **A(1)**; G(2); B(1); G(2); A(4) ... x2

The separations in the pattern are for illustrative purposes to indicate the corner decreases that begin on the following row. They do not occur in the actual beadwork.

45. **nc**; A(1); G(1); B(1); G(2); A(6); G(1); B(1); G(2); A(5); **nc**; A(1); G(1); B(1); G(2); A(5); **nc**; A(1); G(1); B(1); G(2); A(5) ... x2

46. **sc**; A(1); G(2); A(8); G(2); A(6); **sc**; A(1); G(2); A(6); **sc**; A(1); G(2); A(6) ... x2

47. **A(1)**; A(1); G(1); A(9); G(1); A(6); **A(1)**; A(1); G(1); A(6); **A(1)**; A(1); G(1); A(6) ... x2

48. **nc**; A(19); **nc**; A(9); **nc**; A(9) ... x2

49. **sc**; A(18); **sc**; A(8); **sc**; A(8) ... x2

50. **A(1)**; A(17); **A(1)**; A(7); **A(1)**; A(7) ... x2

51. **nc**; A(18); **nc**; A(8); **nc**; A(8) ... x2

52. **sc**; A(17); **sc**; A(7); **sc**; A(7) ... x2

53. **A(1)**; A(16); **A(1)**; A(6); **A(1)**; A(6) ... x2

54. **nc**; A(17); **nc**; A(7); **nc**; A(7) ... x2

55. **A(1)**; G(1); A(2); G(1); A(2); G(1); A(3); G(1); A(2); G(1); A(2); **A(1)**; G(1); A(2); G(1); A(2); **A(1)**; G(1); A(2); G(1); A(2) ... x2

56. **nc**; G(17); **nc**; G(7); **nc**; G(7) ... x2

57. **G(1)**; G(16); **G(1)**; G(6); **G(1)**; G(6) ... x2

BEGIN HEM

58. **nc**; G(17); **nc**; G(7); **nc**; G(7) ... x2

59. **G(1)**; G(16); **G(1)**; G(6); **G(1)**; G(6) ... x2

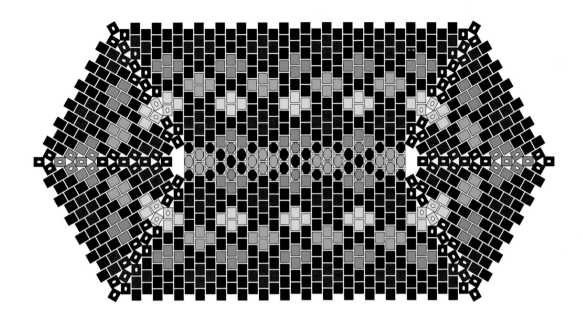

Flat Lid

Flat strip (indicated on the graph as ovals inside of squares)

1 and 2. G(1); D(1); G(2); E(1); G(2); D(1); G(2); E(1); G(2); D(1); G(2); E(1); G(2); D(1); G(1) ... x1

3. D(2); G(1); D(2); G(1); D(2); G(1); D(2) ... x1

4. D(1); G(2); D(1); G(2); D(1); G(2); D(1) ... x1

5. G(2); E(1); G(2); E(1); G(2); E(1); G(2) ... x1

Add end beads.

6. G(1); E(2); G(1); E(2); G(1); E(2); G(1); **G(3)** (end beads) ... x2

7. G(2); E(1); G(2); E(1); G(2); E(1); G(2); G (between end beads); G(1) (between end beads) ... x2

8. F(1); G(2); F(1); G(2); F(1); G(2); F(1); **G(2)**; **F(2)**; **G(2)** ... x2

Begin hexagon increase cycles. From this point on, read the word map as usual, beginning with the corner beads. The long sides will be first.

9. **G(1)**; F(2); G(1); F(2); G(1); F(2); G(1); F(2); **G(1)**; F(1); **F(1)**; F(1) ... x2

10. **nc**; G(1); F(1); G(2); F(1); G(2); F(1); G(2); F(1); G(1); **nc**; G(1); F(1); **nc**; F(1); G(1) ... x2

11. **C(2)**; G(2); C(1); G(2); C(1); G(2); C(1); G(2); **C(2)**; G(1); **F(2)**; G(1) ... x2

12. **C(1)**; C(1); G(1); C(2); G(1); C(2); G(1); C(2); G(1); C(1); **C(1)**; C(1); G(1); **F(1)**; G(1); C(1) ... x2

13. **nc**; C(1); G(2); C(1); G(2); C(1); G(2); C(1); G(2); C(1); **nc**; C(1); G(2); **nc**; G(2); C(1) ... x2

14. **G(2)**; G(1); D(1); G(2); D(1); G(2); D(1); G(2); D(1); G(1); **G(2)**; G(1); D(1); **G(2)**; D(1); G(1) ... x2

15. **G(1)**; G(1); D(2); G(1); D(2); G(1); D(2); G(1); D(2); G(1); **G(1)**; G(1); D(2); **G(1)**; D(2); G(1) ... x2

16. **nc**; G(2); D(1); G(2); D(1); G(2); D(1); G(2); D(1); G(2); **nc**; G(2); D(1); G(1); **nc**; G(1); D(1); G(2) ... x2

17. **G(2)**; E(1); G(2); E(1); G(2); E(1); G(2); E(1); G(2); E(1); **G(2)**; E(1); G(2); **E(2)**; G(2); E(1) ... x2

18. **G(1)**; E(2); G(1); E(2); G(1); E(2); G(1); E(2); G(1); E(2); **G(1)**; E(2); G(1); E(1); **E(1)**; E(1); G(1); E(2) ... x2

19. **nc**; G(1); E(1); G(2); E(1); G(2); E(1); G(2); E(1); G(2); E(1); G(1); **nc**; G(1); E(1); G(2); E(1); **nc**; E(1); G(2); E(1); G(1) ... x2

20. **F(2)**; G(2); F(1); G(2); F(1); G(2); F(1); G(2); F(1); G(2); **F(2)**; G(2); F(1); G(1); **E(2)**; G(1); F(1); G(2) ... x2

21. **F(1)**; F(1); G(1); F(2); G(1); F(2); G(1); F(2); G(1); F(2); G(1); F(1); **F(1)**; F(1); G(1); F(2); G(1); **E(1)**; G(1); F(2); G(1); F(1) ... x2

22. **nc**; F(1); G(2); F(1); G(2); F(1); G(2); F(1); G(2); F(1); G(2); F(1); **nc**; F(1); G(2); F(1); G(2); **nc**; G(2); F(1); G(2); F(1) ... x2

23. **G(2)**; G(15); **G(2)**; G(5); **G(2)**; G(5) ... x2

24. **G(1)**; G(16); **G(1)**; G(6); **G(1)**; G(6) ... x2

Patterns for
Pentagon
Boxes

 # Star

Finished Size: 1¹⁄₂" wide x
    1¹⁄₄" tall (3.8 cm x 3.2 cm)
    without feet

A = Cream; Delica #205;
    370 beads (2 grams)

B = Light Green; Delica #374;
    390 beads (2 grams)

C = Dark Green; Delica #859;
    385 beads (2 grams)

D = Brown; Delica #011;
    1,890 beads (10 grams)

Hem/Inner Wall = Any color;
    360 beads (2 grams)

A   B   C   D

Construction Techniques

For the Base: pages 18–19

For the Sides: pages 24; 26–27

For the Lid with Sides:
    pages 35–36

Base of Box/Lid with Sides

1. **D(1)** ... x5
2. **nc**; C(1) ... x5
3. **C(2)** ... x5
4. **D(1)**; B(1) ... x5
5. **nc**; B(2) ... x5
6. **BDB**; A(1) ... x5
7. **D(2)**; A(2) ... x5
8. **C(1)**; D(1); A(1); D(1) ... x5
9. **nc**; D(4) ... x5
10. **CBC**; C(1); D(1); C(1) ... x5
11. **B(2)**; D(1); C(2); D(1) ... x5
12. **A(1)**; D(1); B(1); C(1); B(1); D(1) ... x5
13. **nc**; D(1); A(1); B(2); A(1); D(1) ... x5

14. **DAD**; D(1); A(1); B(1); A(1); D(1) ... x5

15. **D(2)**; C(1); D(1); A(2); D(1); C(1) ... x5

16. **D(1)**; C(2); D(1); A(1); D(1); C(2) ... x5

17. **nc**; B(1); A(1); B(1); D(2); B(1); A(1); B(1) ... x5

18. **BDB**; A(2); B(1); D(1); B(1); A(2) ... x5

19. **D(2)**; D(8) ... x5

20. **D(1)**; D(9) ... x5

Sides of Box

21. **nc**; D(10) ... x5

22. **D(1)**; D(9) ... x5

23. **nc**; D(10) ... x5

24. **A(1)**; D(4); A(1); D(4) ... x5

25. **nc**; A(1); D(3); A(2); D(3); A(1) ... x5

26. **B(1)**; D(1); A(2); D(1); B(1); D(1); A(2); D(1) ... x5

27. **nc**; D(1); A(3); D(2); A(3); D(1) ... x5

28. **D(1)**; A(1); B(2); A(1); D(1); A(1); B(2); A(1) ... x5

29. **nc**; A(1); B(3); A(2); B(3); A(1) ... x5

30. **D(1)**; B(1); C(2); B(1); D(1); B(1); C(2); B(1) ... x5

31. **nc**; D(1); C(3); D(2); C(3); D(1) ... x5

32. **C(1)**; D(4); C(1); D(4) ... x5

33. **nc**; C(1); D(3); C(2); D(3); C(1) ... x5

34. **B(1)**; C(1); D(2); C(1); B(1); C(1); D(2); C(1) ... x5

35. **nc**; B(1); C(1); D(1); C(1); B(2); C(1); D(1); C(1); B(1) ... x5

36. **A(1)**; B(1); C(2); B(1); A(1); B(1); C(2); B(1) ... x5

37. **nc**; B(1); C(1); D(1); C(1); B(2); C(1); D(1); C(1); B(1) ... x5

38. **B(1)**; C(1); D(2); C(1); B(1); C(1); D(2); C(1) ... x5

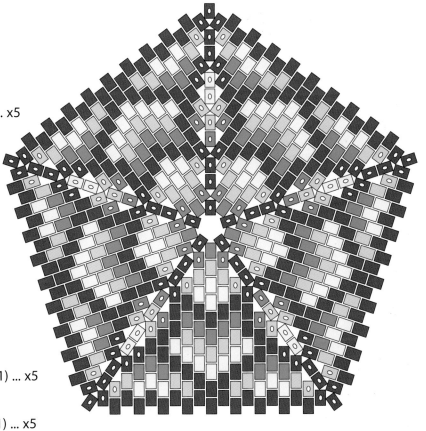

39. **nc**; C(1); D(1); B(1); D(1); C(2); D(1); B(1); D(1); C(1) ... x5

40. **C(1)**; D(1); A(2); D(1); C(1); D(1); A(2); D(1) ... x5

41. **nc**; D(2); A(1); D(4); A(1); D(2) ... x5

42. **D(1)**; D(9) ... x5

43. **nc**; D(10) ... x5

44. **D(1)**; D(9) ... x5

45. **nc**; D(10) ... x5

46. **sc**; D(9) ... x5

47. **D(1)**; D(8) ... x5

48. **D(1)**; D(7) ... x5

49. **nc**; D(8) ... x5

50. **D(1)**; D(7) ... x5

51. **nc**; D(8) ... x5

52. **D(1)**; D(7) ... x5

BEGIN HEM

53. **nc**; D(8) ... x5

54. **D(1)**; D(7) ... x5

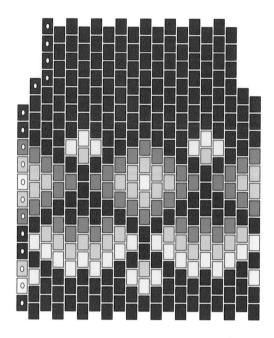

Sides of Lid

21. **nc**; D(10) ... x5

22. **B(1)**; D(4); B(1); D(4) ... x5

23. **nc**; A(1); D(3); A(2); D(3); A(1) ... x5

24. **A(1)**; D(4); A(1); D(4) ... x5

BEGIN HEM

25. **nc**; D(10) ... x5

26. **D(1)**; D(9) ... x5

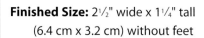 **Flower**

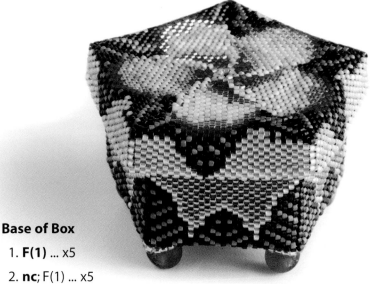

Finished Size: 2½" wide x 1¼" tall (6.4 cm x 3.2 cm) without feet

A = White; Delica #353; 235 beads (2 grams)

B = Pale Pink; Delica #206; 215 beads (2 grams)

C = Medium Pink; Delica #106; 205 beads (2 grams)

D = Rose; Delica #779; 165 beads (1 gram)

E = Light Green; Delica #371; 530 beads (3 grams)

F = Green; Delica #327; 1,340 beads (7 grams)

G = Light Cream; Delica #621; 2,280 beads (12 grams)

H = Dark Cream; Delica #102; 1,280 beads (7 grams)

Hem/Inner Wall = Any color; 660 beads (4 grams)

A   B   C   D   E   F   G   H

Construction Techniques

For the Base: pages 18–19

For the Sides: pages 24; 26–27

For the Lid with Sides: pages 35–36

Base of Box

1. **F(1)** ... x5
2. **nc**; F(1) ... x5
3. **F(2)** ... x5
4. **F(1)**; F(1) ... x5
5. **nc**; E(2) ... x5
6. **EFE**; F(1) ... x5
7. **E(2)**; F(2) ... x5
8. **F(1)**; F(3) ... x5
9. **nc**; F(1); E(2); F(1) ... x5
10. **F(3)**; E(1); F(1); E(1) ... x5
11. **F(2)**; E(1); F(2); E(1) ... x5
12. **F(1)**; E(1); F(3); E(1) ... x5
13. **nc**; F(2); E(2); F(2) ... x5
14. **G(3)**; F(1); E(1); F(1); E(1); F(1) ... x5
15. **G(2)**; G(1); F(4); G(1) ... x5
16. **G(1)**; G(2); F(3); G(2) ... x5
17. **nc**; G(2); F(1); E(2); F(1); G(2) ... x5

18. **G(3)**; G(2); F(3); G(2) ... x5

19. **G(2)**; G(3); F(2); G(3) ... x5

20. **G(1)**; G(4); F(1); G(4) ... x5

21. **nc**; G(10) ... x5

22. **G(3)**; G(9) ... x5

23. **G(2)**; G(10) ... x5

24. **G(1)**; G(11) ... x5

25. **nc**; G(12) ... x5

26. **G(3)**; G(11) ... x5

27. **F(2)**; F(12) ... x5

28. **F(1)**; F(13) ... x5

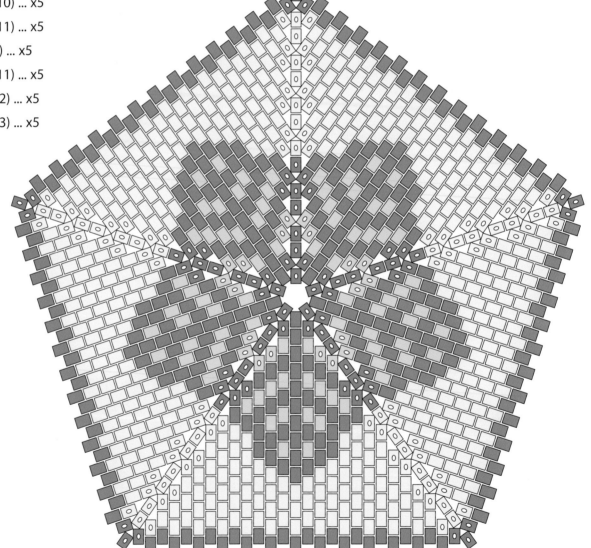

Sides of Box

1. **nc**; E(1); F(1); E(1); F(1); E(1); F(1); E(2); F(1); E(1); F(1); E(1); F(1); E(1) ... x5

2. **F(1)**; E(1); F(1); E(1); F(2); E(1); F(1); E(1); F(2); E(1); F(1); E(1) ... x5

3. **nc**; F(1); E(1); F(3); E(1); F(2); E(1); F(3); E(1); F(1) ... x5

4. **F(1)**; F(1); E(1); F(1); G(1); E(1); F(3); E(1); G(1); F(1); E(1); F(1) ... x5

5. **nc**; E(1); F(1); E(1); F(3); E(2); F(3); E(1); F(1); E(1) ... x5

6. **F(1)**; E(1); F(1); E(1); G(1); F(1); E(1); F(1); E(1); F(1); G(1); E(1); F(1); E(1) ... x5

7. **nc**; F(1); E(1); F(2); G(1); F(4); G(1); F(2); E(1); F(1) ... x5

8. **F(1)**; F(1); E(1); F(1); G(2); F(3); G(2); F(1); E(1); F(1) ... x5

9. **nc**; E(1); F(2); G(1); H(1); F(1); E(2); F(1); H(1); G(1); F(2); E(1) ... x5

10. **F(1)**; E(1); F(1); G(1); H(1); G(1); F(3); G(1); H(1); G(1); F(1); E... x5

11. **nc**; F(1); E(1); F(1); H(2); G(1); F(2); G(1); H(2); F(1); E(1); F(1) ... x5

12. **F(1)**; F(1); E(1); G(1); H(2); G(1); F(1); G(1); H(2); G(1); E(1); F(1) ... x5

13. **nc**; E(1); F(2); H(3); G(2); H(3); F(2); E(1) ... x5

14. **F(1)**; E(1); F(1); G(1); H(3); G(1); H(3); G(1); F(1); E(1) ... x5

15. **nc**; F(2); G(1); H(8); G(1); F(2) ... x5

16. **F(1)**; F(1); G(1); H(9); G(1); F(1) ... x5

17. **nc**; E(1); F(1); H(10); F(1); E(1) ... x5

18. **F(1)**; F(1); G(1); H(9); G(1); F(1) ... x5

19. **nc**; F(1); G(1); H(10); G(1); F(1) ... x5

20. **F(1)**; G(1); H(11); G(1) ... x5

21. **nc**; G(1); H(12); G(1) ... x5

22. **G(1)**; H(13) ... x5

23. **nc**; H(14) ... x5

24. **H(1)**; H(13) ... x5

25. **nc**; H(14) ... x5

26. **H(1)**; H(13) ... x5

27. **nc**; H(14) ... x5

28. **H(1)**; H(13) ... x5

29. **nc**; H(14) ... x5

30. **H(1)**; H(13) ... x5

31. **nc**; H(14) ... x5

32. **H(1)**; H(13) ... x5

BEGIN HEM

33. **nc**; G(14) ... x5

34. **G(1)**; G(13) ... x5

Lid with Sides

1. **G(1) ...** x5

2. **nc**; G(1) ... x5

3. **DG ...** x5

4. **D(1)**; D(1) ... x5

5. **nc**; A(1); D(1) ... x5

6. **DCA**; D(1) ... x5

7. **CA**; D(2) ... x5

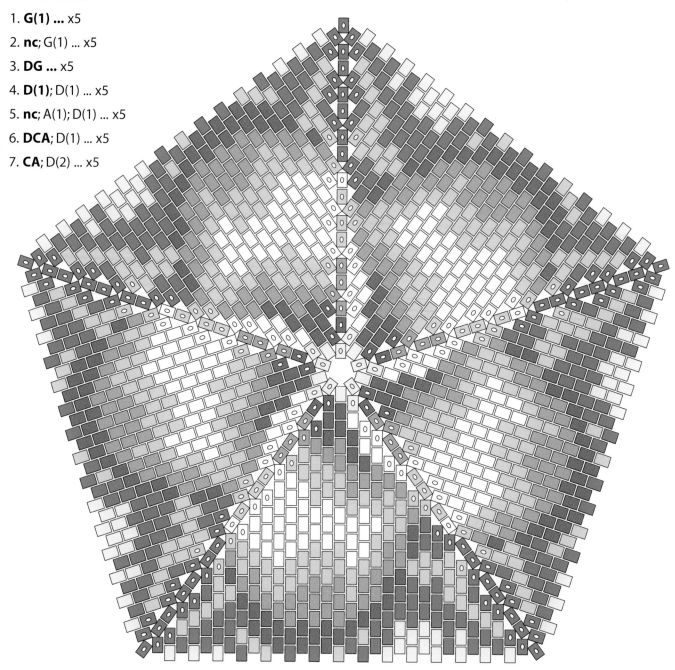

8. **C(1)**; A(1); C(2) ... x5

9. **nc**; A(1); D(1); C(1); B(1) ... x5

10. **BCA**; D(1); C(1); B(1) ... x5

11. **A(2)**; C(2); B(2) ... x5

12. **B(1)**; C(2); B(2); A(1) ... x5

13. **nc**; C(3); B(1); A(2) ... x5

14. **ABB**; B(4); A(1) ... x5

15. **AB**; B(3); A(3) ... x5

16. **B(1)**; C(1); B(1); A(5) ... x5

17. **nc**; F(1); B(1); A(6) ... x5

18. **AAF**; D(1); B(1); A(5) ... x5

19. **BF**; F(1); C(1); B(1); A(5) ... x5

20. **F(1)**; F(1); D(1); C(1); A(1); B(2); A(2); B(1) ... x5

21. **nc**; E(2); C(1); B(1); A(1); B(2); A(1); B(1); C ... x5

22. **EFE**; E(2); C(1); B(6) ... x5

23. **F(2)**; E(2); D(1); C(1); B(4); C(1); D(1) ... x5

24. **F(1)**; E(1); F(2); D(1); C(3); B(2); C(1); E(1) ... x5

25. **nc**; F(1); E(1); F(2); C(1); B(1); C(2); B(1); C(1); E(1); F(1) ... x5

26. **F(3)**; E(1); F(2); D(1); C(5); D(1); E(1) ... x5

27. **F(2)**; E(1); F(3); D(1); C(4); D(1); F(1); E(1) ... x5

28. **F(1)**; E(1); F(4); D(1); C(3); D(1); F(2); E(1) ... x5

29. **nc**; E(1); F(2); G(2); F(1); D(5); F(2); E(1) ... x5

30. **F(3)**; F(1); G(3); F(1); E(1); D(4); E(1); F(2) ... x5

31. **F(2)**; F(3); G(2); F(2); D(3); E(1); F(3) ... x5

32. **F(1)**; G(6); F(1); E(1); F(2); E(1); F(1); G(3) ... x5

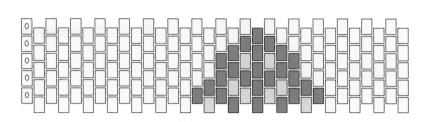

Sides of Lid

1. **nc**; G(7); E(1); F(3); E(1); G(4) ... x5

2. **G(1)**; G(6); F(2); E(2); F(2); G(3) ... x5

3. **nc**; G(7); F(1); E(1); F(1); E(1); F(1); G(4) ... x5

4. **G(1)**; G(7); F(4); G(4) ... x5

5. **nc**; G(8); F(3); G(5) ... x5

6. **G(1)**; G(7); F(1); E(2); F(1); G(4) ... x5

7. **nc**; G(8); F(3); G(5) ... x5

8. **G(1)**; G(8); F(2); G(5) ... x5

BEGIN HEM

9. **nc**; G(9); F(1); G(6) ... x5

10. **G(1)**; G(15) ... x5

 # Dragon

Finished Size: 1¹⁄₂" wide x
1¹⁄₄" tall (3.8 cm x 3.2 cm)
without feet

A = Pea Green; Delica #371;
171 beads (1 grams)

B = Mint Green; Delica #373;
539 beads (3 grams)

C = Teal; Delica #859; 767
beads (4 grams)

D = Purple; Delica #782; 1,829
beads (10 grams)

E = Lavender; Delica #158;
893 beads (5 grams)

F = Pale Yellow; Delica #621;
1,276 beads (7 grams)

G = White; Delica #211; 14
beads

Hem/Inner Wall = Any color;
475 beads (3 grams)

| A | B | C | D | E | F | G |

Construction Techniques

For the Base: pages 18–19

For the Sides: pages 24; 26–27

For the Flat Lid: pages 33–35

Base of Box/Flat Lid

1. **F(1)** ... x5
2. **nc**; F(1) ... x5
3. **F(2)** ... x5
4. **F(1)**; D(1) ... x5
5. **nc**; D(2) ... x5
6. **DFD**; E(1) ... x5
7. **D(2)**; E(2) ... x5
8. **D(1)**; E(1); D(1); E(1) ... x5
9. **nc**; E(1); D(2); E(1) ... x5
10. **E(3)**; E(2); D(1) ... x5
11. **D(2)**; D(1); E(1); D(2) ... x5
12. **D(1)**; D(3); C(1); D(1) ... x5
13. **nc**; C(2); D(1); C(3) ... x5
14. **CCB**; C(3); B(1); C(1) ... x5
15. **CB**; B(2); C(1); B(3) ... x5
16. **B(1)**; A(1); B(1); C(1); B(1); A(1); B(1); C(1) ... x5
17. **nc**; A(2); C(1); B(1); A(2); C(1); B(1) ... x5
18. **B(3)**; A(1); B(1); C(1); B(1); A(1); B(1); C(1) ... x5
19. **BC**; B(3); C(1); B(3); C(1) ... x5
20. **C(1)**; C(1); B(1); C(3); B(1); C(3) ... x5
21. **nc**; D(1); C(3); D(1); C(3); D(1); C(1) ... x5
22. **CDD**; D(1); C(1); D(3); C(1); D(3) ... x5
23. **D(2)**; E(1); D(3); E(1); D(3); E(1); D(1) ... x5
24. **E(1)**; E(2); D(1); E(3); D(1); E(3); D(1) ... x5

25. **nc**; E(1); D(2); E(2); D(2); E(2); D(2); E(1) ... x5

26. **DED**; E(1); D(1); E(1); D(1); E(1); D(1); E(1); D(1); E(1); D(1); E(1) ... x5

27. **D(2)**; D(1); E(2); D(2); E(2); D(2); E(2); D(1) ... x5

28. **D(1)**; F(1); D(1); E(1); D(1); F(1); D(1); E(1); D(1); F(1); D(1); E(1); D(1); F(1) ... x5

29. **nc**; F(2); D(2); F(2); D(2); F(2); D(2); F(2) ... x5

30. **DDF**; D(3); F(1); D(3); F(1); D(3); F(1); D(1) ... x5

31. **F(2)**; F(1); D(1); F(3); D(1); F(3); D(1); F(3); D(1) ... x5

32. **F(1)**; F(15) ... x5

Sides of Box

This pattern is a little different. Although the box has five sides, there is only one dragon. The first word map/pattern "side" actually accounts for one side of the box (the dragon's head) and will be beaded only one time per row. The next four sides (the dragon's body) are identical and will be beaded four times per row. Make sure to bead the "head" on the same side of the box for each row. The lid and base of the box are simply beaded as a pentagon lid and base with identical segments.

1. **nc**; F(16) ... x1
   nc; F(16) ... x4

2. **F(1)**; F(15) ... x1
   F(1); F(15) ... x4

3. **nc**; F(10); D(3); F(3) ... x1
   nc; F(16) ... x4

4. **F(1)**; F(10); D(3); F(2) ... x1
   F(1); F(15) ... x4

5. **nc**; F(1); D(1); F(7); D(1); F(1); E(2); D(1); F(2) ... x1
   nc; F(1); D(1); F(3); D(1); F(3); D(1); F(3); D(1); F(2) ... x4

6. **F(1)**; D(2); F(5); D(4); E(2); D(2) ... x1
   F(1); D(3); F(1); D(3); F(1); D(3); F(1); D(3) ... x4

7. **nc**; F(7); D(2); E(1); D(3); E(1); D(2) ... x1
   nc; F(2); D(2); F(2); D(2); F(2); D(2); F(2); D(2) ... x4

8. **D(1)**; F(1); D(1); F(4); D(1); G(1); E(2); D(2); E(3) ... x1
   D(1); F(1); D(1); E(1); D(1); F(1); D(1); E(1); D(1); F(1); D(1); E(1); D(1); F(1); D(1); E(1) ... x4

9. **nc**; D(2); F(3); D(2); G(1); D(1); E(2); D(2); E(3) ... x1
   nc; D(2); E(2); D(2); E(2); D(2); E(2); D(2); E(2) ... x4

10. **E(1)**; D(1); F(4); D(1); G(1); D(1); E(1); D(1); E(3); D(2) ... x1
    E(1); D(1); E(1); D(1); E(1); D(1); E(1); D(1); E(1); D(1); E(1); D(1); E(1); D(1); E(1); D(1) ... x4

11. **nc**; E(1); F(5); G(2); E(1); D(2); E(2); D(3) ... x1
    nc; E(2); D(2); E(2); D(2); E(2); D(2); E(2); D(2) ... x4

12. **D(1)**; F(1); D(1); F(3); D(3); E(4); D(1); C(2) ... x1
    D(1); E(3); D(1); E(3); D(1); E(3); D(1); E(3) ... x4

13. **nc**; F(1); D(2); F(2); D(1); G(1); D(1); E(1); D(1); E(2); D(1); C(3) ... x1
    nc; D(2); E(1); D(3); E(1); D(3); E(1); D(3); E(1); D(1) ... x4

14. **C(1)**; D(1); E(1); F(1); D(3); G(1); E(1); C(1); D(3); C(1); B(2) ... x1
    C(1); D(3); C(1); D(3); C(1); D(3); C(1); D(3) ... x4

15. **nc**; F(1); E(1); D(3); C(1); D(2); C(2); D(2); C(1); B(3) ... x1
    nc; C(2); D(1); C(3); D(1); C(3); D(1); C(3); D(1); C(1) ... x4

16. **F(1)**; D(2); E(1); C(1); B(1); C(1); D(1); C(1); B(1); C(3); B(1); A(2) ... x1
    B(1); C(3); B(1); C(3); B(1); C(3); B(1); C(3) ... x4

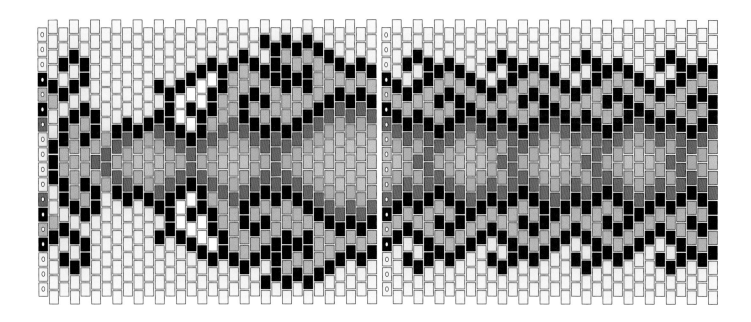

17. **nc**; D(1); E(2); C(1); B(2); C(2); B(2); C(2); B(1);
    A(3) ... x1

    nc; B(2); C(1); B(3); C(1); B(3); C(1); B(3); C(1);
    B(1) ... x4

18. **F(1)**; E(2); C(1); B(1); A(1); B(1); C(1); B(1); A(1);
    B(1); C(1); B(1); A(3) ... x1

    A(1); B(1); C(1); B(1); A(1); B(1); C(1); B(1); A(1);
    B(1); C(1); B(1); A(1); B(1); C(1); B(1) ... x4

19. **nc**; D(1); E(1); C(1); B(1); A(2); B(2); A(2); B(2);
    A(4) ... x1

    nc; A(1); C(1); B(1); A(2); C(1); B(1); A(2); C(1); B(1);
    A(2); C(1); B(1); A(1) ... x4

20. **F(1)**; E(2); C(1); B(1); A(1); B(1); C(1); B(1); A(1);
    B(1); C(1); B(1); A(3) ... x1

A(1); B(1); C(1); B(1); A(1); B(1); C(1); B(1); A(1); B(1);
    C(1); B(1); A(1); B(1); C(1); B(1) ... x4

21. **nc**; D(1); E(2); C(1); B(2); C(2); B(2); C(2); B(1); A(3) ... x1
    nc; B(2); C(1); B(3); C(1); B(3); C(1); B(3); C(1); B(1) ... x4

22. **F(1)**; D(2); E(1); C(1); B(1); C(1); D(1); C(1); B(1); C(3);
    B(1); A(2) ... x1

    B(1); C(3); B(1); C(3); B(1); C(3); B(1); C(3) ... x4

23. **nc**; F(1); E(1); D(3); C(1); D(2); C(2); D(2); C(1); B(3) ... x1
    nc; C(2); D(1); C(3); D(1); C(3); D(1); C(3); D(1); C(1) ... x4

24. **C(1)**; D(1); E(1); F(1); D(3); G(1); E(1); C(1); D(3); C(1);
    B(2) ... x1

    C(1); D(3); C(1); D(3); C(1); D(3); C(1); D(3) ... x4

25. **nc**; F(1); D(2); F(2); D(1); G(1); D(1); E(1); D(1); E(2);
    D(1); C(3) ... x1

nc; D(2); E(1); D(3); E(1); D(3); E(1); D(3); E(1); D(1) ... x4

26. **D(1)**; F(1); D(1); F(3); D(3); E(4); D(1); C(2) ... x1

    D(1); E(3); D(1); E(3); D(1); E(3); D(1); E(3) ... x4

27. **nc**; E(1); F(5); G(2); E(1); D(2); E(2); D(3) ... x1

    nc; E(2); D(2); E(2); D(2); E(2); D(2); E(2); D(2) ... x4

28. **E(1)**; D(1); F(4); D(1); G(1); D(1); E(1); D(1); E(3);

        D(2) ... x1

    E(1); D(1); E(1); D(1); E(1); D(1); E(1); D(1); E(1);

        D(1); E(1); D(1); E(1); D(1); E(1); D(1) ... x4

29. **nc**; D(2); F(3); D(2); G(1); D(1); E(2); D(2); E(3) ... x1

    nc(1); D(2); E(2); D(2); E(2); D(2); E(2); D(2); E(2) ... x4

30. **D(1)**; F(1); D(1); F(4); D(1); G(1); E(2); D(2); E(3) ... x1

    D(1); F(1); D(1); E(1); D(1); F(1); D(1); E(1); D(1);

        F(1); D(1); E(1); D(1); F(1); D(1); E(1) ... x4

31. **nc**; F(7); D(2); E(1); D(3); E(1); D(2) ... x1

    nc; F(2); D(2); F(2); D(2); F(2); D(2); F(2); D(2) ... x4

32. **F(1)**; D(2); F(5); D(4); E(2); D(2) ... x1

    F(1); D(3); F(1); D(3); F(1); D(3); F(1); D(3) ... x4

33. **nc**; F(1); D(1); F(7); D(1); F(1); E(2); D(1); F(2) ... x1

    nc; F(1); D(1); F(3); D(1); F(3); D(1); F(3); D(1); F(2) ... x4

34. **F(1)**; F(10); D(3); F(2) ... x1

    F(1); F(15) ... x4

BEGIN HEM

35. **nc**; F(10); D(3); F(3) ... x1

    nc; F(16) ... x4

36. **F(1)**; F(15) ... x1

    F(1); F(15) ... x4

Patterns for Square Boxes

Tempest

Finished Size: 1½" wide x 1¼" tall (3.8 cm x 3.2 cm) without finial or feet

A = White; Delica # 351; 520 beads (3 grams)

B = Light Blue; Delica # 730; 560 beads (3 grams)

C = Royal Blue; Delica # 864; 664 beads (4 grams)

D = Dark Blue; Delica # 377; 1,148 beads (6 grams)

Hem/Inner Wall = Any color; 428 beads (3 grams)

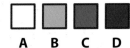

A   B   C   D

Construction Techniques

For the Base: pages 20–21

For the Sides: pages 24; 28–29

For the Flat Lid: pages 33–35

Base of Box/Flat Lid

1. **D(1)** ... x4
2. **nc**; C(1) ... x4
3. **C(3)** ... x4
4. **B(2)**; B(1) ... x4
5. **D(2)**; B(2) ... x4
6. **C(1)**; A(3) ... x3
7. **nc**; D(1); A(2); D(1) ... x4
8. **CBC**; D(1); A(1); D(1) ... x4
9. **B(2)**; C(1); D(2); C(1) ... x4
10. **A(2)**; B(1); D(3); B(1) ... x4
11. **A(1)**; A(1); D(1); C(2); D(1); A(1) ... x4
12. **nc**; D(2); B(1); C(1); B(1); D(2) ... x4
13. **D(3)**; D(1); A(1); B(2); A(1); D(1) ... x4
14. **D(2)**; C(1); D(1); A(1); B(1); A(1); D(1); C(1) ... x4
15. **D(2)**; C(2); D(1); A(2); D(1); C(2) ... x4
16. **D(1)**; C(1); B(1); C(1); D(1); A(1); D(1); C(1); B(1); C(1) ... x4
17. **nc**; C(1); B(2); C(1); D(2); C(1); B(2); C(1) ... x4
18. **CDC**; B(1); A(1); B(1); C(1); D(1); C(1); B(1); A(1); B(1) ... x4
19. **C(2)**; B(1); A(2); B(1); C(2); B(1); A(2); B(1) ... x4
20. **D(2)**; D11 ... x4
21. **D(1)**; D12 ... x4

Sides of Box

22. **nc**; D(1); B(1); A(1); D(1); A(1); B(1); D(1); B(1); A(1); D(1); A(1); B(1); D(1) ... x4

23. **A(1)**; C(1); B(1); A(2); B(1); C(2); B(1); A(2); B(1); C(1) ... x4

24. **nc**; D(1); C(1); B(1); A(1); B(1); C(1); D(1); C(1); B(1); A(1); B(1); C(1); D(1) ... x4

25. **A(1)**; D(1); C(1); B(2); C(1); D(2); C(1); B(2); C(1); D(1) ... x4

26. **nc**; B(1); D(1); C(1); B(1); C(1); D(1); A(1); D(1); C(1); B(1); C(1); D(1); B(1) ... x4

27. **B(1)**; B(1); D(1); C(2); D(1); B(2); D(1); C(2); D(1); B(1) ... x4

28. **nc**; B(1); C(1); D(1); C(1); D(1); C(1); B(1); C(1); D(1); C(1); D(1); C(1); B(1) ... x4

29. **B(1)**; C(1); D(4); C(2); D(4); C(1) ... x4

30. **nc**; C(1); D(1); A(1); D(1); A(1); D(1); C(1); D(1); A(1); D(1); A(1); D(1); C(1) ... x4

31. **C(1)**; D(1); B(1); A(2); B(1); D(2); B(1); A(2); B(1); D(1) ... x4

32. **nc**; D(1); C(1); B(1); A(1); B(1); C(1); D(1); C(1); B(1); A(1); B(1); C(1); D(1) ... x4

33. **D(1)**; D(1); C(1); B(2); C(1); D(2); C(1); B(2); C(1); D(1) ... x4

34. **nc**; A(1); D(1); C(1); B(1); C(1); D(1); A(1); D(1); C(1); B(1); C(1); D(1); A(1) ... x4

35. **A(1)**; A(1); D(1); C(2); D(1); A(2); D(1); C(2); D(1); A(1) ... x4

36. **nc**; A(1); B(1); D(1); C(1); D(1); B(1); A(1); B(1); D(1); C(1); D(1); B(1); A(1) ... x4

37. **A(1)**; A(1); C(1); D(2); C(1); A(2); C(1); D(2); C(1); A(1) ... x4

38. **nc**; A(1); B(1); D(3); B(1); A(1); B(1); D(3); B(1); A(1) ... x4

39. **A(1)**; B(1); C(1); A(2); C(1); B(2); C(1); A(2); C(1); B(1) ... x4

40. **nc**; A(1); C(1); D(1); A(1); D(1); C(1); A(1); C(1); D(1); A(1); D(1); C(1); A(1) ... x4

41. **A(1)**; B(1); D(1); A(2); D(1); B(2); D(1); A(2); D(1); B(1) ... x4

42. **nc**; B(1); C(1); A(3); C(1); B(1); C(1); A(3); C(1); B(1) ... x4

43. **A(1)**; C(1); D(1); A(2); D(1); C(2); D(1); A(2); D(1); C(1) ... x4

44. **nc**; B(1); D(1); A(3); D(1); B(1); D(1); A(3); D(1); B(1) ... x4

45. **B(1)**; C(1); B(1); A(2); B(1); C(2); B(1); A(2); B(1); C(1) ... x4

46. **nc**; C(1); D(1); B(1); A(1); B(1); D(1); C(1); D(1); B(1); A(1); B(1); D(1); C(1) ... x4

47. **B(1)**; D(1); C(1); B(2); C(1); D(2); C(1); B(2); C(1); D(1) ... x4

48. **nc**; C(1); D(1); C(1); B(1); C(1); D(1); C(1); D(1); C(1); B(1); C(1); D(1); C(1) ... x4

49. **C(1)**; D(2); C(2); D(4); C(2); D(2) ... x4

50. **nc**; D(3); C(1); D(5); C(1); D(3) ... x4

51. **C(1)**; D(12) ... x4

BEGIN HEM

52. **nc**; D(13) ... x4

53. **D(1)**; D(12) ... x4

Tomcat

Finished Size: 2" wide x
    2½" tall (5.1 cm x 6.4 cm)
    without feet

A = White; Delica #352;
    1,296 beads (7 grams)

B = Cream; Delica #205;
    357 beads (2 grams)

C = Mustard; Delica #181;
    717 beads (4 grams)

D = Auburn; Delica #773;
    1,381 beads (7 grams)

E = Brown; Delica #769;
    945 beads (5 grams)

F = Turquoise; Delica #861;
    123 beads (2 grams)

G = Green; Delica #274;
    16 beads

Hem/Inner Wall = Any color;
    464 beads (3 grams)

A	B	C	D	E	F	G

Construction Techniques

For the Base: pages 20–21

For the Sides: pages 24; 28–29

For the Lid with Sides:
    pages 35–36

Base of Box

1. **B(1)** ... x4
2. **nc**; B(1) ... x4
3. **CBC** ... x4
4. **C(2)**; C(1) ... x4
5. **C(2)**; C(2) ... x4
6. **C(1)**; C(3) ... x4
7. **nc**; D(4) ... x4
8. **D(3)**; D(3) ... x4
9. **D(2)**; D(4) ... x4
10. **D(2)**; D(5) ... x4
11. **E(1)**; E(6) ... x4
12. **nc**; E(7) ... x4
13. **AEA**; A(6) ... x4
14. **A(2)**; A(7) ... x4
15. **A(2)**; A(8) ... x4
16. **A(1)**; A(9) ... x4
17. **nc**; A(10) ... x4
18. **A(3)**; A(9) ... x4
19. **A(2)**; A(10) ... x4
20. **A(2)**; A(11) ... x4

21. **A(1)**; A(12) ... x4

22. **nc**; A(13) ... x4

23. **A(3)**; A(12) ... x4

24. **A(2)**; A(13) ... x4

25. **A(2)**; A(14) ... x4

26. **A(1)**; A(15) ... x4

27. **nc**; A(16) ... x4

28. **A(3)**; A(15) ... x4

29. **A(2)**; A(16) ... x4

30. **A(2)**; A(17) ... x4

31. **A(1)**; A(18) ... x4

Sides of Box

1. **nc**; A(19) ... x4

2. **A(1)**; A(15); E(1);
   A(2) ... x4

3. **nc**; A(15); E(2);
   A(2) ... x4

4. **A(1)**; A(14); E(1); B(1);
   E(1); A(1) ... x4

5. **nc**; A(5); E(4); A(3);
   E(1); A(1); E(1); B(2);
   E(1); A(1) ... x4

6. **A(1)**; A(1); E(14); B(2); A(1) ... x4

7. **nc**; A(1); E(4); D(4); E(3); B(1); E(1); B(1); E(1); B(1); E(1); A(1) ... x4

8. **A(1)**; E(1); F(2); E(1); D(6); E(1); B(6); E(1) ... x4

9. **nc**; A(1); F(2); E(1); D(7); E(1); C(1); E(1); C(1); E(1); B(1); E(1); A(1) ... x4

10. **A(1)**; E(1); F(1); E(1); D(8); E(1); C(5); E(1) ... x4

11. **nc**; A(1); F(1); E(1); D(3); E(3); D(3); E(4); C(1); E(1); A(1) … x4

12. **A(1)**; E(2); D(3); E(5); D(2); E(3); C(2); E(1) … x4

13. **nc**; A(1); E(1); D(3); E(1); C(1); B(2); E(2); D(4); C(2); E(1); A(1) … x4

14. **A(1)**; E(1); D(3); E(1); C(1); B(4); E(1); D(4); C(1); E(2) … x4

15. **nc**; A(1); E(1); D(2); E(1); C(1); B(5); E(1); D(4); E(1); F(1); A(1) … x4

16. **A(1)**; E(1); D(2); E(1); C(2); B(5); E(1); D(3); E(3) … x4

17. **nc**; A(1); D(2); E(1); C(2); B(6); E(4); C(1); E(1); A(1) … x4

18. **A(1)**; E(1); D(1); E(1); C(2); B(7); E(3); B(1); D(1); E(1) … x4

19. **nc**; E(1); D(2); C(3); B(10); C(1); E(1); A(1) … x4

20. **A(1)**; D(2); E(1); C(2); B(9); C(2); D(1); E(1) … x4

21. **nc**; E(1); D(2); C(3); B(8); C(2); D(1); E(1); A(1) … x4

22. **A(1)**; D(2); E(1); C(3); B(6); E(1); C(1); E(1); D(2); E(1) … x4

23. **nc**; E(1); D(2); C(3); B(3); E(1); B(2); E(4); D(1); E(2) … x4

24. **A(1)**; D(3); C(3); B(3); E(1); B(1); E(1); B(1); E(1); B(1); E(1); D(1); E(1) … x4

25. **nc**; E(1); D(3); C(3); B(1); E(1); B(1); E(1); B(5); D(1); E(1); A(1) … x4

26. **A(1)**; D(3); C(5); E(1); B(1); E(2); B(1); E(1); B(1); E(3) … x4

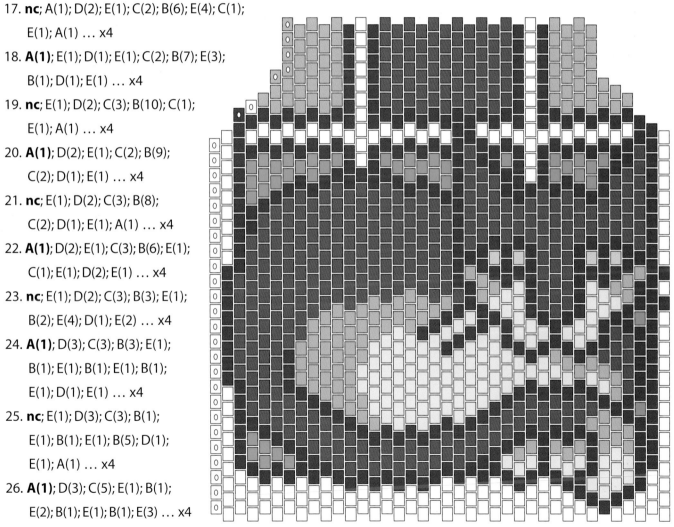

27. **nc**; E(1); D(3); C(5); E(1); B(1); E(1); B(1); E(2); B(1); E(1); F(1); E(1) … x4

28. **A(1)**; D(4); C(5); E(2); B(1); E(1); D(1); E(1); B(1); E(2) … x4

29. **nc**; E(1); D(5); C(4); E(1); B(2); D(2); B(2); E(1); A(1) … x4

30. **A(1)**; D(7); C(1); D(2); C(1); B(1); E(1); D(1); E(1); B(1); C(1); E(1) … x4

31. **nc**; E(1); D(9); E(1); C(1); B(1); D(2); B(1); C(1); E(1); A(1) … x4

32. **A(1)**; D(9); E(1); C(1); E(2); D(1); E(2); C(1); E(1) … x4

33. **nc**; E(1); D(9); C(1); E(2); D(2); E(2); C(1); A(1) … x4

34. **A(1)**; E(1); D(8); E(4); D(1); E(4) … x4

35. **nc**; A(1); D(9); E(1); G(2); D(2); G(2); E(1); A(1) … x4

36. **A(1)**; E(1); D(8); E(4); D(1); E(4) … x4

37. **nc**; A(1); D(10); E(2); D(2); E(2); D(1); A(1) … x4

38. **A(1)**; E(1); D(8); E(1); D(7); E(1) … x4

39. **nc**; A(1); E(1); D(16); A(1) … x4

40. **A(1)**; E(1); D(8); E(1); D(7); E(1) … x4

41. **nc**; A(1); E(1); D(16); A(1) … x4

42. **A(1)**; E(2); D(7); E(1); D(7); E(1) … x4

43. **nc**; A(1); F(1); E(1); D(6); E(1); D(2); E(1); D(2); E(1); D(2); A(1) … x4

44. **A(1)**; E(1); F(1); E(2); D(3); E(3); D(1); E(5); D(1); E(1) … x4

45. **nc**; A(1); F(2); E(6); F(1); D(2); E(3); F(1); D(2); A(1) … x4

46. **A(1)**; E(1); F(3); E(3); F(2); E(1); D(1); E(1); A(1); F(2); E(1); D(1); E(1) … x4

47. **nc**; A(1); F(4); E(2); F(3); D(1); E(3); F(2); E(1); D(1); A(1) … x4

48. **A(1)**; E(1); F(4); A(1); F(3); E(2); F(1); A(1); F(3); E(2) … x4

49. **nc**; A(1); E(9); D(1); E(6); D(1); A(1) … x4

50. **A(1)**; E(5); A(1); E(6); A(1); E(5) … x4

51. **nc**; A(10); E(1); A(6); E(1); A(1) … x4

52. **sc**; E(1); A(8); E(1); A(7); E(1) … x4

53. **sc**; E(17) … x4

54. **E(1)**; E(4); A(1); E(6); A(1); E(4) … x4

55. **A(1)**; C(3); E(2); D(5); E(2); C(3) … x4

56. **nc**; C(4); A(1); D(6); A(1); C(4) … x4

57. **sc**; C(3); E(2); D(5); E(2); C(3) … x4

58. **sc**; C(3); A(1); D(6); A(1); C(3) … x4

59. **C(1)**; C(2); E(2); D(5); E(2); C(2) … x4

60. **C(1)**; C(2); A(1); D(6); A(1); C(2) … x4

61. **nc**; C(2); E(2); D(5); E(2); C(2) … x4

62. **C(1)**; C(2); A(1); D(6); A(1); C(2) … x4

63. **nc**; C(2); E(2); D(5); E(2); C(2) … x4

64. **C(1)**; C(2); A(1); D(6); A(1); C(2) … x4

BEGIN HEM

65. **nc**; C(2); E(2); D(5); E(2); C(2) … x4

66. **C(1)**; C(2); A(1); D(6); A(1); C(2) … x4

Lid with Sides

1. **B(1)** … x4
2. **nc**; B(1) … x4
3. **CBC** … x4
4. **C(2)**; C(1) … x4
5. **C(2)**; C(2) … x4
6. **C(1)**; C(3) … x4
7. **nc**; D(4) … x4
8. **D(3)**; D(3) … x4
9. **D(2)**; D(4) … x4
10. **D(2)**; D(5) … x4
11. **E(1)**; E(6) … x4
12. **nc**; E(7) … x4
13. **AEA**; A(6) … x4
14. **A(2)**; A(7) … x4
15. **A(2)**; A(8) … x4
16. **A(1)**; A(9) … x4
17. **nc**; A(10) … x4
18. **A(3)**; A(9) … x4
19. **A(2)**; A(10) … x4
20. **E(2)**; E(11) … x4
21. **E(1)**; E(2); A(1); E(6); A(1); E(2) … x4
22. **nc**; C(2); E(2); D(5); E(2); C(2) … x4
23. **C(3)**; C(2); A(1); D(6); A(1); C(2) … x4
24. **C(2)**; C(2); E(2); D(5); E(2); C(2) … x4
25. **C(2)**; C(3); A(1); D(6); A(1); C(3) … x4
26. **C(1)**; C(3); E(2); D(5); E(2); C(3) … x4

Lid Sides

1. **nc**; C(4); A(1); D(6); A(1); C(4) … x4
2. **C(1)**; C(3); E(2); D(5); E(2); C(3) … x4
3. **nc**; C(4); A(1); D(6); A(1); C(4) … x4
4. **C(1)**; C(3); E(2); D(5); E(2); C(3) … x4

BEGIN HEM

5. **nc**; C(4); A(1); D(6); A(1); C(4) … x4
6. **C(1)**; C(3); E(2); D(5); E(2); C(3) … x4

 # Shinjin

Finished Size: 1³/₄" wide x
    2¹/₂" tall (4.5 cm x 6.4 cm)
    without finial or feet

A = Cream; Delica #621;
    1,008 beads (6 grams)

B = Burgundy; Delica #103;
    1,428 beads (8 grams)

C = Brown; Delica #011;
    2,848 beads (15 grams)

D = Size 8 beads (any color);
    16 beads

Hem/Inner Wall = Any color;
    284 beads (2 grams)

A	B	C	D
☐	■	■	⬭

Construction Techniques

For the Base: pages 20–21

For the Sides: pages 24; 28–29

For the Flat Lid: pages 33–35

This box has a tiered structure.

Begin each new tier (except the bottom one) in the same way you begin a hem row, but make decreases to complete the tier. The roofs are extensions of the top row of each tier.

Base of Box

1. **C(1)** ... x4
2. **nc**; C(1) ... x4
3. **C(3)** ... x4
4. **C(2)**; B(1) ... x4
5. **B(2)**; B(2) ... x4
6. **B(1)**; C(1); B(1); C(1) ... x4

7. **nc**; C(4) ... x4

8. **C(3)**; A(1); C(1); A(1) ... x4

9. **A(2)**; A(4) ... x4

10. **A(2)**; C(1); A(1); C(1); A(1); C(1) ... x4

11. **C(1)**; C(6) ... x4

12. **nc**; C(1); B(1); C(1); B(1); C(1); B(1); C(1) ... x4

13. **B(3)**; B(6) ... x4

14. **B(2)**; C(1); B(1); C(1); B(1); C(1); B(1); C(1) ... x4

15. **C(2)**; C(8) ... x4

16. **A(1)**; C(1); A(1); C(1); A(1); C(1); A(1); C(1); A(1); C(1) ... x4

17. **nc**; A(10) ... x4

18. **A(3)**; C(1); A(1); C(1); A(1); C(1); A(1); C(1); A(1); C(1) ... x4

19. **C(2)**; C(10) ... x4

20. **B(2)**; C(1); B(1); C(1); B(1); C(1); B(1); C(1); B(1); C(1); B(1); C(1) ... x4

21. **B(1)**; B(12) ... x4

22. **nc**; B(1); C(1); B(1); C(1); B(1); C(1); B(1); C(1); B(1); C(1); B(1); C(1); B(1) ... x4

23. **C(3)**; C(12) ... x4

24. **C(2)**; C(13) ... x4

25. **C(2)**; C(14) ... x4

26. **D(1)**; C(15) ... x4

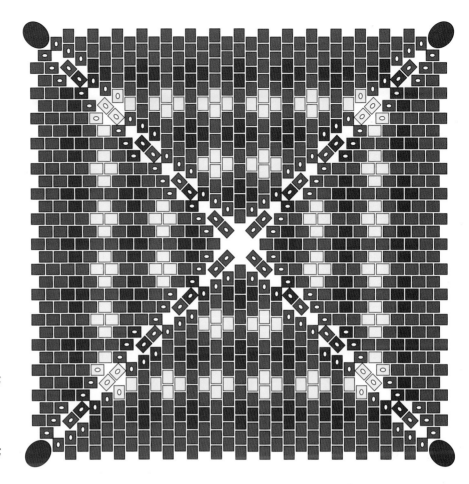

Sides of Bottom Tier

1. **nc**; C(16) ... x4

2. **B(1)**; C(1); B(1); C(1); B(1); C(1); B(1);
   C(1); B(1); C(1); B(1); C(1); B(1); C(1);
   B(1); C(1) ... x4

3. **nc**; **B(16)** ... x4

4. **B(1)**; C(1); B(1); C(1); B(1); C(1); B(1); C(1);
   B(1); C(1); B(1); C(1); B(1); C(1); B(1); C(1) ... x4

5. **nc**; **C(16)** ... x4

6. **C(1)**; A(1); C(1); A(1); C(1); A(1); C(1); A(1); C(1); A(1); C(1); A(1); C(1); A(1); C(1); A(1) ... x4

7. **nc**; A(16) ... x4

8. **C(1)**; A(1); C(1); A(1); C(1); A(1); C(1); A(1); C(1); A(1); C(1); A(1); C(1); A(1); C(1); A(1) ... x4

9. **nc**; A(1); C(2); A(2); C(2); A(2); C(2); A(2); C(2); A(1) ... x4

10. **C(1)**; C(1); B(1); C(3); B(1); C(3); B(1); C(3); B(1); C(1) ... x4

11. **nc**; C(1); B(2); C(2); B(2); C(2); B(2); C(2); B(2); C(1) ... x4

12. **C(1)**; C(1); B(1); C(3); B(1); C(3); B(1); C(3); B(1); C(1) ... x4

13. **nc**; A(1); C(2); A(2); C(2); A(2); C(2); A(2); C(2); A(1) ... x4

14. **C(1)**; A(1); C(1); A(1); C(1); A(1); C(1); A(1); C(1); A(1); C(1); A(1); C(1); A(1); C(1); A(1) ... x4

15. **nc**; A(16) ... x4

16. **C(1)**; A(1); C(1); A(1); C(1); A(1); C(1); A(1); C(1); A(1); C(1); A(1); C(1); A(1); C(1); A(1) ... x4

17. **nc**; C(16) ... x4

18. **B(1)**; C(1); B(1); C(1); B(1); C(1); B(1); C(1); B(1); C(1); B(1); C(1); B(1); C(1); B(1); C(1) ... x4

19. **nc**; B(16); ... x4

20. **B(1)**; C(1); B(1); C(1); B(1); C(1); B(1); C(1); B(1); C(1); B(1); C(1); B(1); C(1); B(1); C(1) ... x4

21. **nc**; C(16) ... x4

22. **C(1)**; C(15) ... x4

Sides of Middle Tier

Bead row 1 exactly as you would bead the first hem row.

The skipped corner is considered an "**sc**."

1. **sc**; C(15) ... x4

The next six rows use Steps 3, 4, 5, 1, 2, and 3 of a square-box decrease cycle (pages 28–29). You will then resume tubular peyote stitch.

2. **C(1)**; C(14) ... x4

3. **A(1)**; C(1); A(1); C(1); A(1); C(1); A(1); C(1); A(1); C(1); A(1); C(1); A(1); C(1) ... x4

4. **nc**; A(14) ... x4

5. **sc**; C(1); A(1); C(1); A(1); C(1); A(1); C(1); A(1); C(1); A(1); C(1); A(1); C(1) ... x4

6. **sc**; C(12) ... x4

7. **B(1)**; C(1); B(1); C(1); B(1); C(1); B(1); C(1); B(1); C(1); B(1); C(1) ... x4

8. **nc**; B(12) ... x4

9. **B(1)**; C(1); B(1); C(1); B(1); C(1); B(1); C(1); B(1); C(1); B(1); C(1) ... x4

10. **nc**; C(12) ... x4

11. **C(1)**; A(1); C(1); A(1); C(1); A(1); C(1); A(1); C(1); A(1); C(1); A(1) ... x4

12. **nc**; A(12) ... x4

13. **C(1)**; A(1); C(1); A(1); C(1); A(1); C(1); A(1); C(1); A(1); C(1); A(1) ... x4

14. **nc**; C(12) ... x4

15. **B(1)**; C(1); B(1); C(1); B(1); C(1); B(1); C(1); B(1); C(1); B(1); C(1) ... x4

16. **nc**; B(12) ... x4

17. **B(1)**; C(1); B(1); C(1); B(1); C(1); B(1); C(1); B(1); C(1); B(1); C(1) ... x4

18. **nc**; C(12) ... x4

19. **C(1)**; A(1); C(1); A(1); C(1); A(1); C(1); A(1); C(1); A(1); C(1); A(1) ... x4

20. **nc**; A(12) ... x4

21. **C(1)**; A(1); C(1); A(1); C(1); A(1); C(1); A(1); C(1); A(1); C(1); A(1) ... x4

22. **nc**; C(12) ... x4

23. **C(1)**; C(11) ... x4

Sides of Top Tier

Bead row 1 exactly as you would bead the first hem row. The skipped corner is considered an "**sc**."

1. **sc**; C(11) ... x4

The next six rows use steps 3, 4, 5, 1, 2, and 3 of a square-box decrease cycle.

You will then resume tubular peyote stitch.

2. **C(1)**; C(10) ... x4

3. **A(1)**; C(1); A(1); C(1); A(1); C(1); A(1); C(1); A(1); C(1) ... x4

4. **nc**; A(10) ... x4

5. **sc**; C(1); A(1); C(1); A(1); C(1); A(1); C(1); A(1); C(1) ... x4

6. **sc**; C(8) ... x4

7. **B(1)**; C(1); B(1); C(1); B(1); C(1); B(1); C(1) ... x4

8. **nc**; B(8) ... x4

9. **B(1)**; C(1); B(1); C(1); B(1); C(1); B(1); C(1) ... x4

10. **nc**; C(8) ... x4

11. **C(1)**; A(1); C(1); A(1); C(1); A(1); C(1); A(1) ... x4

12. **nc**; A(8) ... x4

13. **C(1)**; A(1); C(1); A(1); C(1); A(1); C(1); A(1) ... x4

14. **nc**; C(8) ... x4

15. **B(1)**; C(1); B(1); C(1); B(1); C(1); B(1); C(1) ... x4

16. **nc**; B(8) ... x4

17. **B(1)**; C(1); B(1); C(1); B(1); C(1); B(1); C(1) ... x4

18. **nc**; C(8) ... x4

19. **C(1)**; A(1); C(1); A(1); C(1); A(1); C(1); A(1) ... x4

20. **nc**; A(8) ... x4

21. **C(1)**; A(1); C(1); A(1); C(1); A(1); C(1); A(1) ... x4

BEGIN HEM

22. **nc**; C(8) ... x4

23. **C(1)**; C(7) ... x4

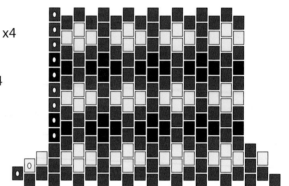

You will now add first the middle and then the bottom roof. Begin a new thread, and weave through the appropriate tier until your needle exits the last (top) row of the tier. (This row is indicated by the grey beads in the diagram.) You will then add one row without increasing (the corner will be a down bead) and then perform one square-box increase cycle.

Middle Roof

1. **nc**; B(12) ... x4
2. **B(3)**; B(11) ... x4
3. **B(2)**; B(12) ... x4
4. **C(2)**; B(13) ... x4
5. **D(1)**; C(14) ... x4

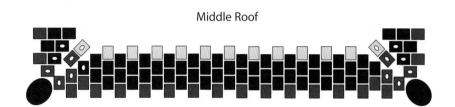

Middle Roof

Bottom Roof

1. **nc**; B(16) ... x4
2. **B(3)**; B(15) ... x4
3. **B(2)**; B(16) ... x4
4. **C(2)**; B(17) ... x4
5. **D(1)**; C(18) ... x4

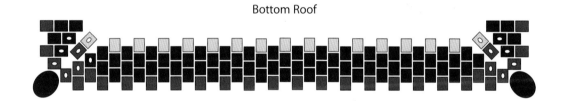

Bottom Roof

Flat Lid

1. **C(1)** ... x4
2. **nc**; C(1) ... x4
3. **C(3)** ... x4
4. **C(2)**; B(1) ... x4
5. **B(2)**; B(2) ... x4
6. **B(1)**; C(1); B(1); C(1) ... x4
7. **nc**; C(4) ... x4

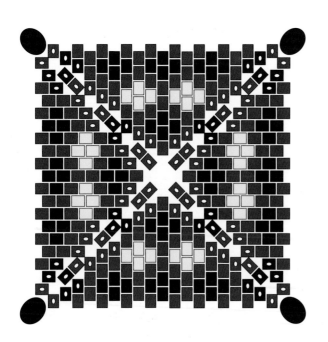

8. **C(3)**; A(1); C(1); A(1) ... x4

9. **A(2)**; A(4) ... x4

10. **A(2)**; C(1); A(1); C(1); A(1); C(1) ... x4

11. **C(1)**; C(6) ... x4

12. **nc**; C(1); B(1); C(1); B(1); C(1); B(1); C(1) ... x4

13. **B(3)**; B(6) ... x4

14. **B(2)**; C(1); B(1); C(1); B(1); C(1); B(1); C(1) ... x4

15. **C(2)**; C(8) ... x4

16. **D(1)**; C(9) ... x4

Blank Graph Worksheets
for Your Original Designs

Triangle Base and Lid

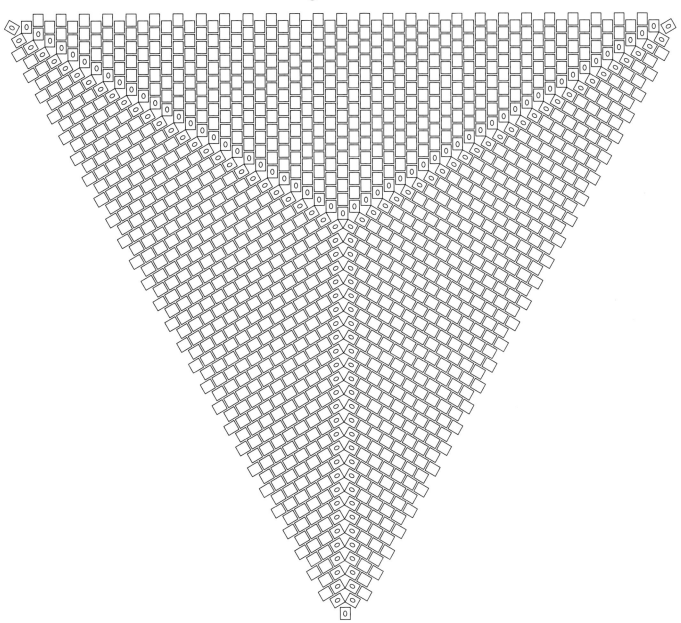

Hexagon Base and Lid

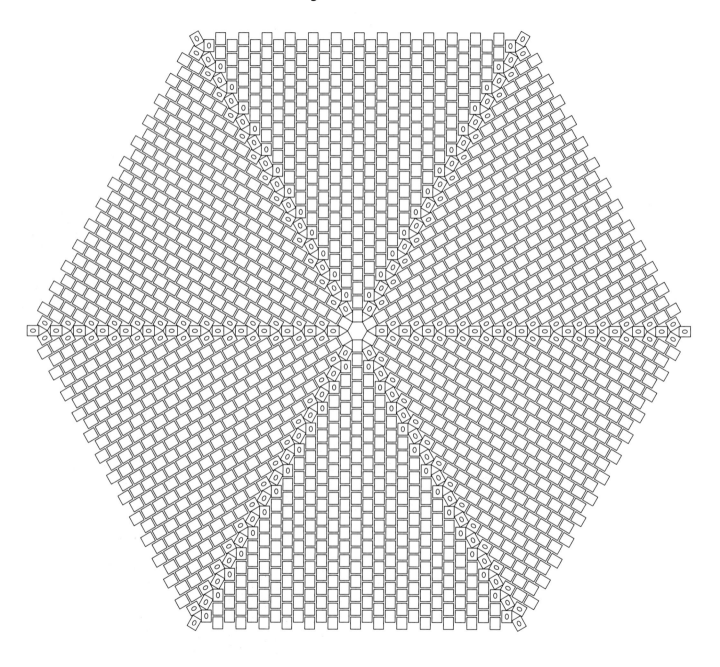

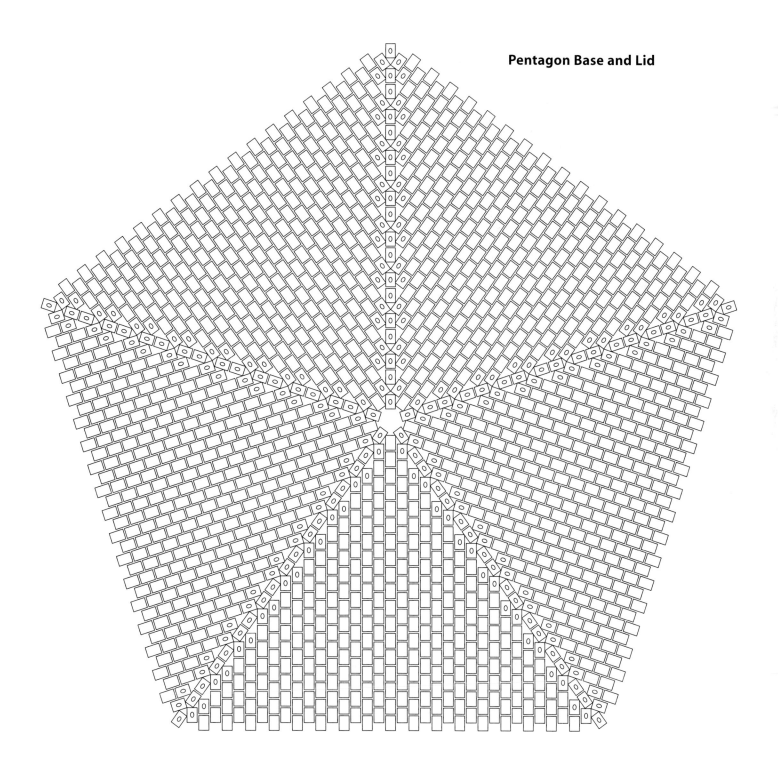

Pentagon Base and Lid

Square Base and Lid

Oblong Hexagon Base and Lid

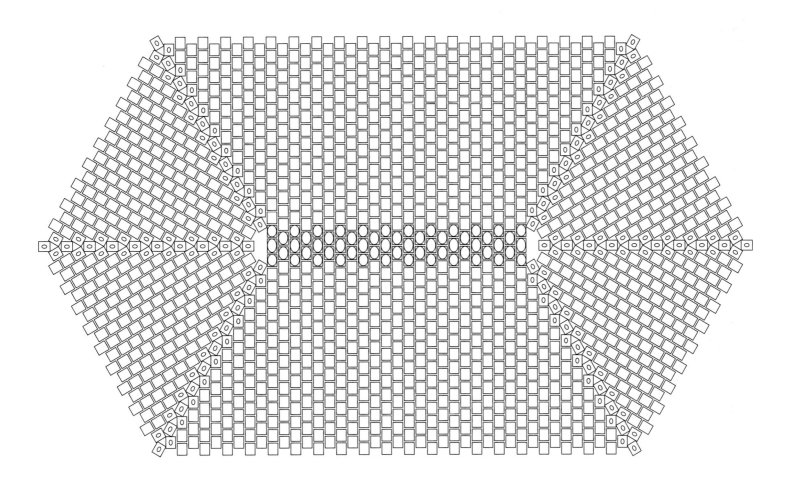

Oblong Square Base and Lid

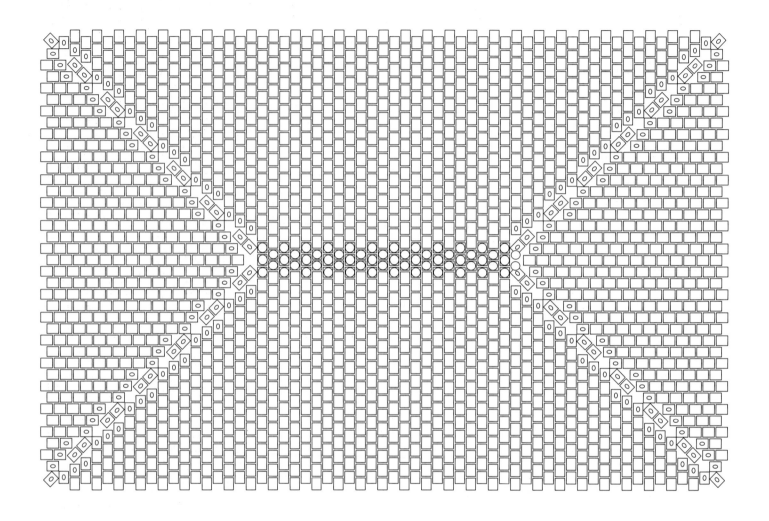

Worksheet for All Box Sides

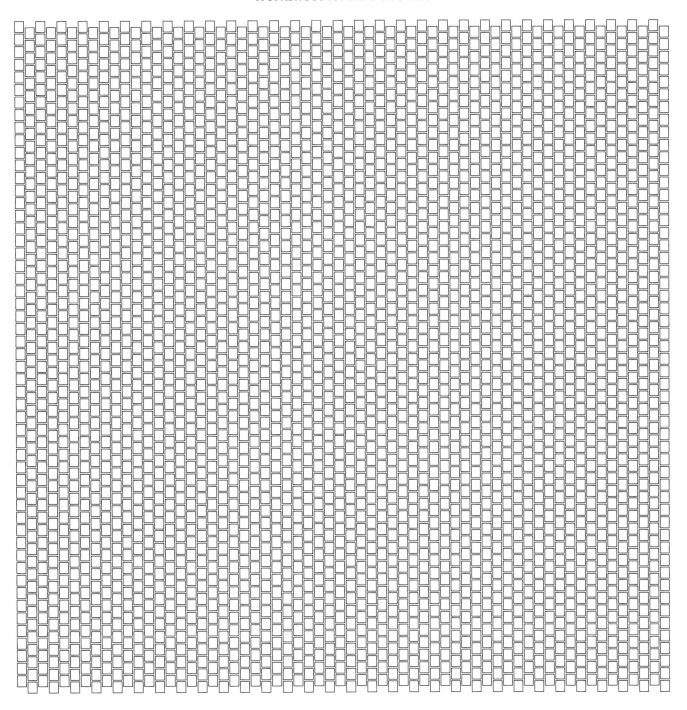

Index